Enjoy the Read!

From Cotton Fields to Mission Fields

The Anna Knight Story

DOROTHY KNIGHT MARSH

ISBN: 978-1-4834-6024-6 (sc)
ISBN: 978-1-4834-6023-9 (hc)
ISBN: 978-1-4834-6025-3 (e)

Library of Congress Control Number: 2016917300

Lulu Publishing Services rev. date: 11/17/2016

Introduction

*A*s great nieces of Anna Knight, we are all still in awe of her as a person. As children, some of us were afraid of her because of the stern look on her wrinkled face when she talked to us. But, underneath that sternness was a woman who deeply cared about her family and wanted us to live up to the Knight Family name.

My husband Elliott and I were living in Atlanta, Georgia when my cousin Lewis Booth called from Huntsville, Alabama saying, "Dorothy they have moved all of Anna Knight's belongings out of the house that she was sharing with Miss Trula Wade, and you should come and get the information and keep for the family.

I was full of excitement and joy as I drove to Huntsville to retrieve the items. Lewis met me at the house that Anna and Miss Wade shared, which was next to the campus market area. I had a feeling that I will never forget as we began our search crawling underneath the house to explore a shallow space. It was in June 1988. There were boxes filled with all kinds of papers, documents, clothing and other personal items along with an old trunk. We sorted out the information belonging to Anna Knight from other boxes that were placed under the house, gathered as much as we could and placed them in the back of my Jeep. It took most of the day.

Driving back to Atlanta, I remembered my freshman year as

a student at Oakwood Academy. It was my first experience away from my parents. I stayed in Henderson Hall, the dormitory for academy girls. Even though I had grown up on the Oakwood campus, boarding there was a new experience for me. My parents moved to Chicago and my brother Curley and I stayed in the dormitory on the campus of Oakwood. Anna asked Miss Wade to place me in a room on the first floor next to her until I could get accustomed to living alone in the dorm. She kept an eye on me and sometimes would ask me to come to her apartment and have dinner with her. She made the best potato salad which was and is my favorite food. I will never forget spending time with her and enjoying her company.

After retrieving the papers, documents, boxes and the trunk, I felt as if I had been on a treasure hunt. In a way I had, looking back at the boxes stacked high in the back of the Jeep; it felt as if I had been given a part of history that had been lost for a long time. Night after night when sorting through the boxes I could not believe the information that each one contained. I decided right then that the information should be shared with the rest of the world. I was not quite sure how to go about doing it, until I found her hand written draft copy of her autobiography, *The Mississippi Girl*. Tears filled my eyes. This was the answer. I will re-write the book and incorporate the new information taken from her personal papers and records and interviews newly found. It was the perfect opportunity to share her life story. Talking about the potential project with others generated excitement and encouraged me to write this book.

However, once I started to write, despite my strong motivation, "life" got in the way. After retiring in the fall of 2011 from Washington, DC, we moved to my birthplace, Soso, Mississippi. Finally, I had the time to really get serious and complete the book project.

So the journey began, my sister Florence Blaylock and I continued to keep her memory and legacy by sharing her life story with schools and churches. We discussed and examined the life of this young "green girl" from Mississippi, not knowing where this journey was taking us. After our presentations, we left people wanting to know more about the life of this remarkable woman. Now you have it here in this book, *From Cotton Fields to Mission Fields, The Anna Knight Story*.

The Childhood Years

Chapter 1

"Will some of the cousins please write to me and send me some reading matter?" That was Anna Knight's plea in 1891 in rural Mississippi. She was desperately trying to connect with people outside of her community.

On a warm spring day in April 1856 there stood a beautiful mulatto woman, the wind gently blowing her long wavy hair and her beautiful glaring green eyes stared into space as she stood on the auction block in New Augusta, Mississippi. She stood there with her children, holding one child in her arms and another with her small arms wrapped tightly around her legs.

She was in her teens and pregnant. There was fear in the young mother's eyes, not knowing who would buy her, or if she would be allowed to keep her children. It was the custom in those days to take the mother and give the small children away to someone else. This beautiful woman's name was Rachel, Anna Knight's grandmother. The baby in her arms was Georgeann, Anna's mother. The small child with her arms wrapped around Rachel's leg was Rosette. Not much in known about this child.

After a few rounds of bidding, a tall and wealthy white horse trader and farmer, Jackie Knight, purchased Rachel. But; she cried so much that he decided to purchase the children too. He took them to his plantation in Jasper County Mississippi. He had purchased a large tract of virgin land. It was beautiful, untouched territory in Jasper County, in the southern part of Mississippi known as the Pine Belt; it had plenty of pine trees, lakes, streams and wild game. A few months after moving to the plantation of Jackie Knight, Rachel gave birth to a son she named Jeffery. She adored her children and was willing to do everything to protect them. Jackie Knight's grandson Newton (Newt) Knight bought a large tract of land that he wanted to homestead. After emancipation, Newton persuaded Rachel, Georgeann, Rosette and Jeffery to move on his land which was on the edge of Jasper County. Although he did not believe in slavery he needed help establishing his farm. Rachel and her children were no longer slaves, but they were very poor and had no other means of survival. They were compelled by economic circumstances to work the land as sharecroppers.

After a few years of sharecropping, Rachel's children were becoming adults and she wanted her own land and home. Newt deeded her a 160- acre tract of land with the understanding that she had to work to clear it and make it suitable for farming. Rachel and her children were accustomed to hard work; however, this was their own land. Cutting down trees, and building fences, cultivating the soil to grow crops were jobs they were happy to do.

Newton Knight was married to Serena Turner a neighbor from Jasper County, and together they had a family of nine children. Rachel and her family lived nearby. Serena noticed that Newt was attracted to Rachel and was spending a lot of time with her. Serena had enough of his disrespect, so she left Newt and went to live with their daughter Mollie. At that time it was against the law for a black person and white person to marry. Newt Knight made his own laws and no one questioned him, so he and Rachel had a common law marriage. They had seven children. After Rachel's death, Newt became involved with Georgeann, Rachel's daughter by another white man, and they had four children, one of which was Rachel "Anna" Knight.

By hard work and frugality, Georgeann, Anna's mother, was able to purchase eighty acres of land at fifty cents per acre from the government. It was near Gitano, Mississippi, six miles north of the nearest post office that was located in Soso, Mississippi. With the help of others in the small community, Georgeann cleared the land and built a one-room, hewn-log house with a porch on one side for a kitchen. Later she built a separate kitchen cabin; the porch was partitioned, and one half was used as a room for young Anna and her brother Howard. The other half was used as a veranda. They loved to sit on the veranda to watch for wild turkeys and deer in hopes that they could catch them and have food during the winter months.

The family was finally making a life for themselves by steadily working and sharecropping, and they saved money until they were finally able to purchase a cow, a horse and a yoke of oxen. Her father Newt would come by and give them a hand when needed. After a few years of working, Georgeann was able to homestead another eighty acres of land. She knew that owning land was a way of providing for her family, who now owned 160 acres with plenty of virgin timber. Their land provided all the necessities of life as they knew it. They grew their own food, planted cotton and sold timber for cash crop.

Soon the log cabin home that Georgeann had built for her family was getting too crowded. Georgeann, Anna, her brother Howard and sisters Grace and Lessie all lived in the house together with her uncles, (some of whom were married), and with other family members. The living conditions were not the best and life was always a struggle. There was always work to be done in the fields, keeping the house or babysitting the small children. Anna felt she was "always in the way", and she was constantly shoved and pushed around. She spent most of her time in nature, walking through the woods, enjoying the ponds, and eating wild berries, nut grass and other fruits to satisfy her hunger. She developed a love for the outdoors because that was where she had her own space to run and jump and play without bumping elbows with other members of the family.

There were no idle hands in her family, and everyone had chores. When Anna reached the age of eight, her chore was to make sure that water was in the house at all times. That meant she had to go to the spring, get the water, carry it to the house and fill all the buckets. She also carried water to those who were working in the fields. She learned very early in life to work wherever she was needed. When she was older, she took her place in the fields with the rest of the family members.

As with any large family farm in those days, when everything was done by hand, there was little time for pleasure. One of the exciting events in the spring and summer was to join other families in the community and go to the creek and swim, especially on a hot day after working in the fields. The men and the women did not swim together, but went on alternate days. On one of those outings, the children were so anxious to go; that they ran ahead of the adults.

This particular creek was known for quicksand. Anna's mother and brother warned them to be careful where they jumped in because a swimmer could get caught in the quicksand. Anna, being the adventurous one in the group, swam out farther than the others. As she was splashing in the creek her foot suddenly touched the quicksand -- and it quickly sucked her down. The rest of her family was standing on the bank of the creek and frantically called to her mother, "Help save Anna, she is going to drown!" Her mother jumped into the creek with her clothes on and waited until the wave rolled Anna up; then she grabbed Anna's arm and

4

slowly but firmly pulled her out to safety and laid her on the bank of the creek.

When Georgeann saw that her daughter was all right, she gave her a hug and a good lecture. She told her, "This is the cost for being disobedient but, you must not be afraid of the water. We will go back into the creek and I will teach you how to swim." That day Anna learned two valuable lessons, how to swim and the importance of obedience.

At an early age, Anna knew that field work was not for her. She was not satisfied with that way of life and wanted to go to school to learn to read and write. The children in the community went to school for a short period in the summer and winter because during other times all hands were needed to work the farms. It was baffling to her why she could not attend school like the rest of the children in the community given that she looked just like them. But because of her mixed heritage and being a child of Newton Knight, she was not accepted. With a thirst for knowledge and determination, Anna visited her white cousins who lived about a mile away. They were very friendly to her, and she often spent the night with them. They shared their books with her and, as she'd hoped, she was beginning to read. In exchange for the girls teaching Anna to read, her mother sewed and did laundry for the family. Anna helped the girls with their chores. When they were finished with Noah Webster's, *Blue Backed Speller*, they gave it to Anna. Oh how she treasured that book. It was the first book that she ever owned and she did not let it out of her sight. Later she was able to get *McGuffey's Reader, Book Four*, she took it with her wherever she went, studying and sounding out the words as best she could. She'd then go to the creek bed, smooth out sand, and practice forming the letters in the sand with her finger or with a stick. On Sundays, when she would go to play with the children in the community in Six Town; or to her cousins' house, the books were tucked under her arm like a gift package. She gathered groups together, both children and adults, to have spelling bees. Soon she became an expert in reading, spelling and writing.

Religion was not a big part of her childhood. The only time the family went to church was once a month when the circuit preachers would come to the church. The Presbyterian minister came through the community twice a year, the hard shell Baptist minister visited once a month. The Mormons were always present, talking to the people in the community, and some of the family converted to the religion. The church was for the whites in the community but they allowed the black families to attend and sit in the back of the church. Her mother liked going to the church meetings. Anna who was eight years old at the time attended with her mother, mainly to see what the women were wearing and who the new neighbors were. Anna with her limited knowledge did not believe all of their preaching, especially about hell fire. She could not believe something could burn forever and never burn up. The preachers did not use their Bibles much; they picked out one text and preached their own ideas mainly that if you sinned you would go to hell and burn forever. They never talked about the forgiving grace of God. The Methodist preachers would come out of the pulpit and put their hands on the children's forehead and say "God Bless the babes." Anna did not like that.

Anna sat and watched this for some time. She finally decided that she would create her own church. She and other children would go to the oak grove where they could not be seen or heard. They used bark from the trees as hymnals, they sang the songs from memory. Anna preached about hell fire as though she believed in it, and urged the members to come forward if they wanted to escape damnation, and then she prayed for them. The younger children gave her their little hands in repentance. They really thought they were like the adults who worshiped in their church.

Soon she became tired of playing church and was getting restless for something else exciting to do with her time. The family traveled to the town of Shubuta to sell the cotton and to buy supplies. On one of the trips, Anna got the bright idea to build her own town. The railroad was being built and that was when she saw the tall telegraph poles that carried telegraph wires. She decided to have a telegraph system in her town, with the help of the other children, they used long sticks for the poles, strings for the telegraph wire, and at the age of twelve she became mayor of her town. Looking around her little town, she thought that something was missing, a school. They made a little school on the gallery of her family's log cabin. Anna at the age of fourteen was the teacher, since she was the only one who could read and write. She guessed from what she'd learned that she had about a sixth grade education. The school consisted of four pupils, her younger cousins, who she taught for six weeks in the summer, during the period when nothing could be done in the fields. To make the blackboard, they took two one foot by four feet boards, nailed them together, stood them against the long cabin, painted them with wet soot and let them dry in the sun. To make the chalk, they went to the reed brake and dug out natural white chalk from the mud banks, chips of wood served as books, blocks of wood were their chairs. She wrote the alphabet on the primitive blackboard and asked the students to repeat the letters. Using the Webster speller and a reader that she bought in Shubuta with her earnings from the cotton crop, she pronounced the words, and they repeated the words and spelled them from memory. Using the sand for paper, and a twig from a nearby tree for a stylus, the children formed the letters in the sand. This little school was the only education that the children received and it lasted for two years.

Georgeann saw to it however, that Anna could not spend all of her time with the school or the town that she and the others had built. There was always plenty of work to be done. Wool and cotton had to be carded into rolls to spin for knitting stockings and clothing; Anna's work was to operate the loom which was large and occupied a lot of space in the house. In the summertime, it was moved to the veranda. By the time she was thirteen years old, she took her place behind the plow. Cultivating the fields was her favorite thing to do. She loved to see the rich soil turning over and knowing that plants would grow there soon.

Sundays were always special times, especially in the afternoon. Anna and the children played games, indulged in spelling bees, softball games, arrow shooting and old-fashioned sing- a- longs from a book called *The Sacred Harp*. On Sundays her mother prepared big dinners and other family members stopped by to visit and eat. Their home was always open and they did not mind sharing meals with others in the community.

Part of the family farm was wooded and had to be cleared by hand. Trees were cut with a crosscut saw and ax. The wood was cut into boards and split rails. Whenever a neighbor needed some extra rails to split or logs to roll, it was the custom for them to invite all his friends to come and give a day's work. The women of the community set up their quilting frames and had a quilting bee on the same day. The quilting bee was the only non-labor occasions where women could gather and exchange gossip. They baked their favorite dishes, chicken and dressing, turkey or sometimes they killed a hog or sheep. If it was a good work day, a dance would follow.

The nearest railway town Ellisville, was twenty-eight miles from their farm, and took few days by ox wagon to make the round trip. They did not get to town often to pick up food and supplies they mostly lived off the land. Six miles from their farm was Soso, a small town where the post offices, water-powered gristmill, sawmill and a country store was located. Mail was delivered by horseback in saddle bags once a week. Anna and her family carried their corn in a sack on horseback to the mill to get a supply of corn meal for the month. Many times she walked the six miles with her mother and brother Howard, and carried a dozen eggs or a few chickens to trade for sugar and coffee. Those were truly simple times and pioneering days. Her family was not rich or educated, but they were blessed with all that they needed. They owned their 160-acre farm, cows, horses, and sheep and grew their own food. Food was simple; cornpone made with salt and water only, and cooked in a Dutch oven or skillet was a staple. Anna and her brother Howard vowed when they grew up, they would never eat corn bread for breakfast again.

Not many people outside the community visited Six Town. But one day an agent came to their home soliciting subscriptions for a periodical called *The Home* and *Fireside Magazine*. With it, he gave several oil print pictures as a bonus, two large ones of George and Martha Washington and several smaller ones. Anna had never seen anything so beautiful in her life, and really wanted the magazine. Her mother had a dollar, but not for anything like that. Anna begged for the magazine and the beautiful pictures until her mother gave in and placed the subscription. After the man left their home, Anna's mother scolded her for carrying on about the magazines and told her she was never to do anything like that again.

The magazines and the bonus pictures finally arrived. Every month Anna received *The Home* and *Fireside Magazine,* she had never seen anything so beautiful. The pictures were placed on the wall, anyone who visited their home, could not miss seeing them. Although her mother could not read, she enjoyed looking at the pictures, and on Sunday night she liked hearing Anna read stories to her from *The Home and Fireside Magazine*. Some would make her cry, others made her angry, but still she read the stories and they became more and more fascinating.

Once in while there was beautiful script writing in the magazines, so she took the magazines, spread them out on the smooth sand and practiced writing in the sand until she had mastered the script writing. She did not have the funds to purchase paper and pencil to write, but the sand worked just fine.

One day as she was reading the magazine and noticed an advertisement stating that if someone would send ten cents, their name would be published in a dictionary and they would receive free samples of books, papers, and catalogues. She managed to scrape together ten cents and had a friend write the letter because she had never written a letter before. When she received the magazine the next month, Anna saw her name printed in the book, she was proud and showed it to her brother and sisters. Soon she was receiving a variety of books and pamphlets, and sample paper.

Among the many sample magazines sent to her, one was called *"Comfort"* published in Augusta, Maine. At the top of the front page she saw that it cost twenty-five cents a year for the subscription. Anna knew that she had to have the paper, so she picked cotton to earn the money and this time wrote her own letter to subscribe to the paper. The paper featured a column called "The Cousins Exchange" in which people made requests for items, and if anyone in the Exchange had the items they would send it to them. Anna looked over the column carefully and found one request that suited her. It read, "Will some of the cousins please send me some nice reading matter? I would like to correspond with someone of my own age." Anna thought this would be good for her and she copied the request exactly as it read, signed "Anna Knight, age 18" (although she was only sixteen). Within a few weeks, the little post office in Soso was flooded with mail for

Anna Knight. This was in the spring of 1891. No one in the entire county got as much mail! All sorts of books and papers were sent, such as *Buffalo Bill, Wild Bill, Jesse James, Peck's Boy* and many others. There was a set of books, *The King's Daughters, The Ram's Horn*, and other religious papers were sent to her. After a while her correspondence slowed because it was hard to afford the postage to mail the letters.

To her surprise forty people responded to her request for reading material and correspondence. One of the people responding was Miss Edith Embree of Oakland, California, and W. W. Eastman, of Texas. Mr. Eastman sent her a large bundle of papers containing *The Review and Herald, Youth's Instructor, Sabbath School Worker,* and the *Medical Missionary.* She did not know these people but, she knew they were Christians. Later she discovered that they were Seventh-day-Adventists. Miss Embree worked for the Signs of the Times publishing house, and took a special interest in Anna and kept up the correspondence. Her office had a Young People's Literature and Correspondence bank, and she took Anna's name from the *"Comfort"* paper and each week sent a copy of the *Signs of the Times* to her.

Anna had a wide selection of books and papers, she read the cheap novels and story books first. Three of them made a deep impression on her young mind. In her later years she warned all young people to leave all the cheap reading alone.

Anna soon became bored reading the novels and the cheap stories. On Sundays or when she had idle time, instead of reading; she'd take her revolver and ride her pony up and down the hills pretending she was chasing Indians. She practiced shooting at knots on trees and at other targets. Like her father, who could shoot a deer with one eye closed, Anna became a good markswoman, hitting the mark at fifty or a hundred yards away. She and her pony spent a lot of time together and she had trained him to turn, stop or run at the motion of her hand.

The magazines and cheap novels did not interest her anymore. She decided to concentrate on the *Signs of The Times*, tracts and books sent by Miss Embree. Anna noticed that there was something special about the papers that Miss Embree sent her. They were very clean and of high quality. Her letters had even margins, no mistakes and very pretty penmanship. Every paper Miss Embree sent had some articles marked with a red or blue "X" and in the letters which followed, she told Anna to be sure to read those articles because they had been a help to her and she hoped that they would help Anna as well. Miss Embree also requested that she write back and tell her what she thought about the topics that she had marked. Anna carefully tried to imitate her writing when she responded to her letters. When she asked questions or tried to argue about some ideas, Miss Embree wrote only a little about it and say, "I am sending you a tract on that very topic which will tell you all about what you want to know. If you still don't understand, ask again and I will be glad to try to help you." This inspired Anna to do three things: read the papers more thoroughly; think about what she had read; and write back with her understanding of the topic. Since there was no electricity in the house, to read at night, Anna gathered pine knots for the fire and sat by the fireplace for light.

On Friday and Saturdays, Georgeann and the family went to the grist mill in Soso to get their corn milled. On the way back home, she stopped by the post office to pick up the mail. There was always a bundle of mail for Anna. There was nothing she enjoyed more than to spend most of the day on Sunday in the woods reading and studying the information that was sent to her by Miss Embree. She picked out certain topics to discuss with the circuit preachers who visited the community. She knew that they could not explain or understand the information that she had read, but that was a mind game that she liked to play with them.

Observing Saturday as a day of rest and worship instead of Sunday was a question the circuit preachers could not answer and would not discuss. They only said, "There are some jumbled-up people out there who are crazy." The idea of keeping Saturday for Sunday is absurd." But, Anna could not get the question out of her mind, so she wrote Miss Embree, asking her to explain it to her in depth. Anna liked to argue in those days, because she thought she knew everything. After all, she was the one who could read and spell. She wrote a letter to Ms. Embree and asked her, "How can you prove that Saturday was the seventh-day of the week?" By return mail she received a thirty-two page letter quoting scriptures, chapter and verse.

It was a good thing she did because Anna didn't have a whole Bible. There was only half of the Bible in her house and the book of Revelation was missing. Her brother Howard told her that their uncle had a whole bible, but he may not let her read it. Anna struggled with trying to read the Bible texts in order to answer all the questions that she had in the material.

In all the correspondence that she had written to Miss Embree, she never once revealed her living conditions or anything personal about herself. She would write about the county where she lived, the cotton, sugar cane, peanut crops that they grew and bragged about the good life they had enjoyed, but never a word about the log cabin they lived in, having no school, nor that she was of mixed heritage. She lived in those letters, and forgot about her surroundings and all the things she did not have.

Anna plowed the cotton and corn fields, it was very hard work for a young girl. But she knew that soon she could take a break and have time to read the magazine she slipped in her pocket to read. About mid-day, she took her break. She sat on the ground by a fence under a tree, taking the magazine out of her pocket to read, instead of talking or joking with the other members of her family. Sometime they worked in groups of six to eight and while the others chewed tobacco and told wild stories, Anna was reading silently to herself. After about a half an hour of rest to cool off from the heat and humidity, they continued their work in the fields until dusk.   The family was buying a farm and they had to work on shares. Most of the farm land they owned was cleared but they were purchasing another forty acres and homesteading another eighty. They had acquired one hundred and sixty acres.

It took about six months for Anna to understand and accept all the information she was reading. Miss. Embree sent her Bible instructions and lessons along with the *"Steps to Christ"* book. It was brand new with a pretty red cover, and divided into subjects so Anna could easily find the exact topic she wanted. When all the work and chores were done for the day, Anna made a fire in the fireplace, burning the pine knots that were gathered earlier. When the fire was bright enough for reading, Anna and her mother sat by the fireplace and she read to her from the *Steps to Christ* until her mother would fall asleep.

Anna was convinced that the new information she was reading was true and she had to live according to those teachings. The only problem was that there was not a church in her community that taught or practiced those beliefs. Somehow she had to find out more, not knowing that her search for the truth would lead her to worlds unknown.

Seeking an Education

Chapter 2

Mississippi was always known to have storms and tornados. In late summer a terrible tornado passed through the community about three miles from Anna's house. Some of the people lost their homes, others were injured and a few lives were lost. Sometimes during the storms, Anna stayed in the log cabin alone and very frightened. She did not know how to pray but held the Bible tightly in her hand feeling that in some mysterious way she was safe. After the storm was over, Anna went outside to see the devastation that was done in her community. She was very upset about the lives that were lost and wondered if she had been killed, would she have been saved. She worried about this for a few days, then finally one Sunday she went to see her aunt who was not more than a year older than her who had joined the Baptist Church. Anna thought that she should know more about the Bible. The two of them went to a field of broom straw. They found a good spot and sat down and looked up texts in the Bible as the straw gently swayed back and forth around them. Anna was not satisfied with the information that they found and thought that she should get her Bible and study for herself. Night after night she stayed up, reading the Bible searching to find the answer to her question, "If she had been killed in the storm, would she have been saved?"

After hours of studying, Anna came to the conclusion that if she wanted to be saved she had to change the way she was living. She decided that night to live differently and to ask for God's help. She had never prayed anything but the Lord's Prayer, but that night she prayed a prayer straight from the heart. Anna made up her mind that she would stop using bad language, going to dances and live up to all that she knew about the new religion. She also knew that it was not going to be easy.

The next week there was a "big working" day; a day that everyone in the community harvested their crops and lay by the land for the winter months. Following the day of work, a dance was usually held and all the young girls and young boys dressed up in their finest to attend the dance and card party. Anna's cousins and friend asked if she was going to attend, at first she said no, but they begged her so much that she finally decided to go. She told them, however, that it would be her last one.

Anna was always the life of the party; she was the one who led everyone into the dances. As they were having a merry time, it began to thunder and lighting. The rain was coming down so hard that the dance stopped and the people were afraid. While they were waiting for the rain and the wind to stop, Anna used the time to tell them about what she had been reading which was bringing about a change in her life. She also told them that this was going to be the last dance that she would attend; they had to find another way to celebrate and have fun if they wanted her to take part in it. They all thought that she was crazy and continued in their way of celebration, but Anna did not participate in their activities anymore.

During the winter months there was not any work in the fields that needed to be done, all the crops had been harvested and food had been put away for the winter months. Anna now had the time to correspond with Edith Embree more frequently. She studied every piece of literature that was sent to her and what she did not understand she wrote Edith Embree to get answers to her questions. She felt that she needed to learn more about the information that she was studying. Not having a complete Bible of her own made it difficult to search the scriptures to find the answers and the truth about what she was reading. Her uncle had a complete Bible that he never used, so she asked him if he would let her use it. He said, "If you will pick two hundred pounds of cotton, I will give you the Bible." "Alright I will do it" Anna said. So she picked the cotton and before she realized it, she had made the two hundred pounds. True to his word, her uncle gave her the Bible.

She quickly finished her chores for the day, helped her mother cook supper and hurried to clean the kitchen. Now it was finally the time that she had been looking forward to all day, the time to unwind and study the Bible. She gathered fat pine knots and piled them high in the corner to make sure that a good fire was in the fireplace that night. When most of her family had gone to bed, she took her reading material and sat on the floor by the fireplace and read for hours. She did this on most nights sometimes crying because the message was so beautiful. She did not know how to pray but again she prayed a prayer from her heart the best that she knew how. Anna did not know the name of the religion that she was studying, but, she knew that she should try to live her life according to the Bible and all the other information that she had learned. Miss Embree saw that Anna was interested in the materials sent to her because of the questions that she was asking. She thought that it was time for Anna to make contact with someone who lived close to her. A letter was sent to I. Dyo Chambers of Chattanooga, Tennessee who at the time was secretary-treasurer of the Southern Missionary Tract Society and Book Depository in Chattanooga, Tennessee. She asked him to contact a young girl in Mississippi by name of Anna Knight.

A few weeks later she received a letter from Brother Chambers introducing himself to her. In his letter were also copies of more reading materials for her to study. He also told her that he was a Seventh-day Adventist and sent her a Sabbath School lesson quarterly appropriate for her age and other reading materials easy for her to understand. Anna still did not know anything about the Seventh-day Adventist religion, but she knew that it was the way she wanted to live her life. Even though she had gone to churches with her family, she felt that something was missing; the preachers seemed to scare people into the church by telling them how terrible "hell" was. From the articles and books that had been sent to her and studying the Bible, she knew that were other truths that she must learn about. Praying in earnest to God, Anna decided that she was going to keep Saturday as the Sabbath in accordance with all the information that she had been studying. She then decided that she wanted to be baptized.

At that time the whole South was a mission field. Adventism had not reach Mississippi until 1898. In Vicksburg, the Morning Star a paddle wheeler steamboat, captained by Edison White and following instructions from his mother, Ellen G. White had become the center of comprehensive ministry to freed slaves and sharecroppers. Each week they gathered from miles around to attend the classes and lectures and worship services aboard the steamboat

Until she could figure out a way to get baptized, she had to do what was expected of her at home. She worked very hard during the week making sure that the wood was cut and any other chores were done It was winter time and there was not much work they could do in the fields, but living on a farm, there was always something to do.

By this time, they had built another small house which was the kitchen and eating area. There was a long porch that reached from the kitchen area to the big house which was the living and sleeping area. On Saturdays, Anna cooked the breakfast, made sure there was fresh water in the house, the beds were made and the floors clean. She made sure her two sisters Lessie and Grace were up fed and dressed for the day. After all of this was done, she took her mail and Bible and went into the woods to study.

With her dog, a big black German shepherd by her side, she spent the whole day in the woods eating nuts and berries and reading. Her dog kept watch and did not allow a hog or cow to get near her. She enjoyed the peace and quiet of the woods. She listened to the birds singing and the tall pines trees gently swaying; she admired the beautiful fall colors of the trees. On rainy days it was really difficult for her to stay in the house, her mother argued with her the whole day because Anna would not do any work on Saturday.

It was December, Anna felt that she had studied enough and was sure that she wanted to be baptized and accept this new religion. She wrote brother Chambers and told him that she wanted to be baptized. After several letters, Brother Chambers invited her to come to Chattanooga, Tennessee. He did not know if she was colored or white because it was never mentioned in all of their correspondences. Anna was worried about what her mother would say. She knew she would not give her permission to go. When her family was told about her decision to go to Chattanooga to be baptized, they did everything they could to discourage her. They said that one cannot believe everything they read in the papers and that people are not that kind. After all, she had never been out of the Jasper county community before. They put all kinds of horror stories in her mind, such as, "People don't know what or who you are, you are just a young girl traveling alone and anything could happen to you. Where are you going to get the money to make the trip?" Furthermore, no one has contacted me to ask my permission." Still, Anna made up her mind and decided she was going, but she promised that she would return by planting time to help make the crops for the next year if they would allow her to go. The plan was for her to go to Chattanooga to spend the winter months January and February, and return home in time to help with the planting of the crops for the next year. Mr. and Mrs. Chambers thought that Anna should attend school while she was staying with them; they made arrangements for Anna to attend the Graysville School. They agreed to pay for the tuition if Anna could pay the railway fare to get to Chattanooga. Finally her family agreed to let her go on the condition she returned to help with the spring planting. Anna agreed and was then able to go. Soon she would be of age to do whatever she wanted to do. Anna wrote a letter to Mr. Chambers and told him she would be coming and advised him of the day that she would arrive. She also asked how she would recognize him, since they had never met. Brother Chambers sent her a picture of him and told her to have a *Review and Herald* magazine in her hand when she got off the train so he would recognize her.

Anna and her brother Howard had a bale of cotton together that they took to the gin to sell. She received her half of the bale of cotton which was about twenty-three dollars, and used the money to buy her round trip ticket on the train to Chattanooga to meet Brother and Sister Chambers. It was a bold step for a sixteen year old young girl from the farm in Mississippi, but she knew that this was something she had to do. After hearing about Anna's pending trip to Chattanooga, her father, who was white, said to her, "I don't believe in your going off, but since your head is set, don't let those folks know that you have any money. If they don't treat you right, come home. When you get up there, they are going to ask you if you are a Negro, tell them you are not, because you are not. A Negro means a black man, and you are not black, so you will be telling the truth."

Anna always had the highest regard for her father, even though he had three families, one with his white wife Serena, and another with Rachel who was deceased and the other with her mother Georgeann. It was known in Jones and Jasper County that her father Captain Newt Knight lived openly among his mixed race community. The people who lived in the community were called "White Negros", Anna was one of them

The day finally arrived for the trip to Chattanooga. Her mother had mixed feelings about her daughter going away by herself and meeting someone who she had never met before. She gave Anna a hug and said, "You be back in time for planting the crops." This was the first time that she had left her home, family and community, let alone to catch a train by herself. She was nervous about taking this journey but Anna knew that this was something she had to do. She gave her sisters, Grace and Lessie a big hug and kisses and started on her journey to Chattanooga. Howard hooked up the wagon, placed Anna's small suitcase in the back and they traveled to Ellisville to catch the train. Anna and Howard and another one of her cousins arrived in plenty of time for Anna to buy a roundtrip ticket and get a coconut for her lunch. It was three hundred and eighty- two miles to Chattanooga, Tennessee. Anna was nervous and excited. This was going to be an adventure for her. Anna hugged her brother and cousin and boarded the train. As the train made its way along the tracks rocking from side to side, passing through small towns, Anna looked out the window in amazement. She had never been away from home before. The train seemed to take forever to reach Chattanooga—winding around Lookout Mountain was a little scary for her, but she was on a mission.

After finally reaching the train station in Chattanooga, Anna quickly grabbed the *Review and Herald* magazine to hold in her hand just as she was told. Brother Chambers and his wife true to their word met her at the train station. Brother Chambers saw Anna with the magazine in her hand and immediately went to her. "Are you Anna Knight for Mississippi" he asked. "Yes," Anna replied. They welcomed her with open arms and took her to their home. She spent two months with them, yet they did not ask if she was white or colored.

It was Christmas break and a Week of Prayer was being held at their church. She attended the meetings every night and listened to every word. When the call came to join the church, Anna raised her hand to be baptized. On a cold sleeting and rainy day, Anna was baptized in the cold water in a creek with two other young people. It was a day she will never forget. Her heart was so full of joy she wanted to tell everybody how wonderful she felt.

The next Monday morning Brothers Chambers took her to Graysville Academy to enroll in school. Graysville Academy was a small school started by Professor George Colcord and his wife, who used their own money to rent a room above a General Store in Graysville, Tennessee. The first year they had twenty-three students enrolled and tuition was $12.50 a month. The school is known today as Southern Adventist University in Collegedale, Tennessee.

Brother Chambers paid the first month. The students had to work to help defray the cost of the tuition and books. The first day she attended class; the other students in the class looked at her and began to whisper about her. Anna knew that there was going to be trouble. The students told their parents about the new person in the school that looked a little strange to them. The parents went to the principal of the academy and told him they heard that a "nigger" had been allowed to attend the school. They told Mr. Colcord that they would not stand for it at Graysville Academy. They decided that if she was not taken out, they would mob her. The next day Elder Colcord, the principal, called her to his office and asked her some questions. They asked if she was a "mulatto". She said no, and that she didn't know what a mulatto was. She followed her father's advice and told them what he told her. "When they asked who you are, just say nothing." Looking surprised and bewildered, Elder Colcord told her that since the people were angry, she had better wait until he could find out who she was. They asked for the names of persons they could write to find out if she was telling the truth. They said that they had no doubt of what she said, but would like to have references which they could present to those who objected to her presence. She gave them some names to write to; white folk who she knew were her friends. Of course, they never replied to their letters. Anna knew they would not.

There was no more talk about the incident, but Anna did not return to school. However, she remained at Graysville Academy, roomed with the matron of the school, helped her with her work, and was taught privately until the time came for her to return home. She had learned so much in those ten weeks than anyone at home could ever dream of. She never told anyone of her disappointment at the school, although it was deep and bitter. The members of the church were very kind and welcomed her at the church on Sabbath. It was then that she made up her mind that nothing would change her and she was going to do everything she could to make sure that the truth and education reached her people. She did not want anyone to experience what had happened to her because of the ignorance of a few people. It was going to be her main goal the rest of her life to teach and educate everyone that she came in contact with, especially her family at home.

As promised, when spring came, she returned to Mississippi and helped plant the crops. She did not tell her family about the incident at the school for fear that they would say "I told you so." Her family and others could see the change in her. They began to question her. They started saying that she was crazy, and that those people had put a spell on her. It became impossible to keep the teachings of her new religion at home. On Saturdays after she prepared the breakfast and did her daily chores, she went to her favorite place in the woods. Taking her Bible, revolver and her faithful dog by her side, she spent the day reading and meditating and praying that someday she would be able to worship in peace.

It was time for cotton chopping. Plenty of grass had grown in the fields, and this was when the real trouble came between her and the family. Anna was told to go and help work in the fields. She refused at first, but her mother said:

"You go and plow the cotton,"

"No," she replied.

"You will do what I say as long as you live under my roof" her mother said sternly.

She had never disobeyed her mother before and felt bad about it. With tears in her eyes she plowed the field just as she was told to do. She felt that she had committed the unforgiveable sin. The horse could sense her frustration as they raced through the four acre field before the sun went down. That Sunday, she did not go to church with the rest of the family, instead she stayed home and worked in her flower garden. Later, she wrote a letter to Brother Chambers telling him of her ordeal and asked if she would be forgiven. He replied telling her that she would be forgiven, because she was under age and should obey her mother. During the rest of the year, there were many other situations that made it almost impossible for her to stay in her mother's house. One day, Anna had a very bad argument with her mother. She was told that if she did not give up her religion, she would have to leave the house. Anna agonized and prayed about what her mother said and made the decision to leave home. She continued to help her mother and family harvest the crops and at the end of the season, Anna made her plans to return to Chattanooga. At dinner that evening, she told her family that she was leaving Mississippi so that she could get an education and serve God in peace. Her mother was not surprised at Anna's decision and told her if this is what you must do, do it with all your heart and soul, but don't expect any help from her. Howard was upset because he and Anna were very close, but he understood and told her not to forget about them. Lessie and Gracie had tears in their eyes. They did not want to see their sister leave. A week later Anna packed her one suitcase, took her share of the money received from selling cotton, and made her plans to return to Chattanooga. Upon arriving at the train station in Ellisville, Howard told Anna, "You take my share; I hope it will help you." Anna hugged him tightly because she did not know when she would see him again, and boarded the train.

Chapter 3

The following morning the train pulled into the station at Chattanooga, Tennessee. The sun was shining so beautiful but cold. She looked out the window to see if Brother Chambers was there waiting for her. After scanning through the crowd of people on the platform, she finally saw him with a broad smile on his face and holding a black cape with quilted satin lining that Mrs. Chambers had made for her. It was the most beautiful cape that Anna had ever seen. As he handed the cape to her, she quickly put it on to cover her country dress and to shield herself from the keen cold wind.

When they reached the home of the Chambers, his wife met them at the door and gave Anna a big hug. "Come right in and make yourself at home. We have two other girls here, but there is always room for one more" said Mrs. Chambers.

Anna felt as if she had known them all of her life. They were so kind to her. Her eyes were red and swollen from loss of sleep and crying on the train the night before. She remembered the tender way her brother said goodbye to her. She had left the only home she had ever known. Not knowing when she would see her mother or the rest of her family, Anna began to cry again. Realizing that she had given up everything to get an education, there was no turning back. So she quickly adjusted to the new surroundings and met her new friends as warmly and as cheerfully as possible. This was December, one year after her first visit to Tennessee, at which time she was baptized and became a Seventh day Adventist. Anna was still a little homesick and missed her family. She occasionally wrote home to tell them how she was doing, but never received letters in return. Mrs. Chambers purchased beautiful material on sale and acquired the assistance of a dressmaker to make clothes for Anna. Within a short period of time Anna had a few nice suits and dresses to wear to church and other meetings.

The Chamber's home was always open to visitors. Elder G. A. Irwin, the superintendent of the Southern Mission Field, lived at Mt. Vernon, Ohio, but traveled to the South frequently to visit companies and churches in various cities. He always stayed with Brother and Sister Chambers, since they had once lived in Ohio and both men served as soldiers in the Union army during the Civil War. The Chambers told Elder Irwin about Anna, how she had left home because she had found a new way of life and wanted to get an education to become a teacher. They also told him about the experience at Graysville School. Elder Irwin suggested that they send her to Mt. Vernon Academy in Ohio, because he was sure that no questions would be asked and she could attend school there. The Chambers discussed this with Anna to see how she felt about it. At first Anna was a little hesitant. She had just left Mississippi and now to go farther away to Ohio was a bit uncomfortable. She needed some time to think about it. Anna wrote a letter to her mother telling her of her plans to attend Mt. Vernon Academy in Ohio. She did not get a reply. Nevertheless she felt her mother should know where she was.

Everyone thought this would be an answer to their prayers. Anna was a little worried because she still was the timid girl from Mississippi. Ohio was further away from home, but, if this was the only way that she could get an education, then she was willing to try it. Anna had not received any type of formal education. What she had learned was self-taught and from her cousins who let her read their school books. Mr. Chambers knew she needed tutoring and taught her at night or during the day when he had free time to prepare her for the academy at Mt. Vernon.

For nine months from the time that she arrived in Chattanooga in December to September of the next year Anna tried to learn everything that she could so that she would be able to keep up with the rest of the class. She was ahead in some of the studies but behind in others, especially in grammar and math. In the meantime, Graysville Academy principal Mr. Colcord tried to persuade the Chambers to let her return to Graysville Academy. However, Anna had not forgotten the experience she had there, and felt that she would have a better chance at Mt. Vernon, so decided to go there instead.

Mrs. Chambers was a milliner and dressmaker and also a good baker. She was president of a women's club called the "Women's Exchange". The group baked whole-wheat bread, pies, cookies, and cakes and also made needlework to sell. They had made arrangements with the stores on Market Street in Chattanooga to sell their goods. Sometimes they worked in the stores to help sell the goods. This was a very profitable venture for the ladies and they were proud of their work.

Mrs. Chambers specialized in salt-rising bread. She was up at four o'clock in the morning and stayed up until ten o'clock in the evening baking sixty loaves of bread. Anna helped by taking the bread to the Exchange daily for her. Mrs. Chambers also taught her how to bake the bread, but would not let her do all the baking without her supervision.

Later she learned that she did all of this hard work of baking and selling the bread to buy clothing for her to take to Mt. Vernon Academy. Mrs. Chamber made her a beautiful hat to replace her old worn feathered hat, new suits and dresses for church, and for school. Each time an outfit was finished; she spread it carefully on the bed and said, "Anna, I hope this will last you until the Lord comes." Anna was overjoyed with the beautiful clothing and promised to take good care of them. The unselfish love and sacrifice of Mrs. Chambers made a lasting impression on Anna, and she never forgot it.

One day she was so overwhelmed by all the nice things that Mrs. Chambers was doing for her, that she could no longer hold back the tears. She went to the attic to have a good cry and did not want Mrs. Chambers to see her. But, Mrs. Chambers went to the attic to look for her and found her curled up on the floor crying. She tenderly put her arms around Anna.

"Have you had bad news from home?" Mrs. Chambers asked.

"No," replied Anna.

"Are you homesick?"

Again Anna replied, "No."

"Have I hurt your feelings?" Mrs. Chambers asked.

"No." Anna said.

"Then what is the matter my dear?" Mrs. Chambers asked.

Anna told her that she was thinking of all the nice things she had done for her, and that she was just a poor girl from Mississippi who had nothing to give in return for all the kindness that she had given her. Mrs. Chambers hugged her close and told her something she would never forget:

> *"You Dear Child, we don't expect any pay for what we are doing for you. We believe you will make a worker in God's cause someday, and if we should sleep before Christ comes, our work will go on through you. We have helped many girls get started in the Lord's work, and we are glad to be able to help you."*

That was in 1894, and from that day, Anna never forgot the faith Mrs. Chambers had in her to succeed. Anna was more determined than ever to get an education and to make Brother and Sister Chambers proud of her. Until her death she never forgot the love and kindness that was shown to her by the Chambers.

By September, Anna was ready for school. She had worked with Mrs. Chambers doing whatever needed to be done. She saved and solicited funds to attend Mt. Vernon Academy, and for clothing. She was happy to attend the first real school in her life, not counting the one day at Graysville Academy. The Chambers took her to the train station. As Anna boarded the train for Mt. Vernon, Ohio, she couldn't help but think about her family in Mississippi now that she was farther away from her home. She still had not received any letters from her mother. Anna felt that they had forgotten about her. Although she was carrying this heavy burden in her heart, there was also joy in knowing that she was finally getting her wish to get an education.

Mt. Vernon Academy was a beautiful campus. She had never seen anything like it in her young life, and she knew it was going to be hard to keep up with the rest of the students in the class, but all she could do was to try her best. During a math class one day, everyone was a little irritated with her because the whole class period was spent trying to get Anna to understand the problem. The teacher was patient and showed her each step. The class was excused and the teacher asks her to remain. She knew that he was going to be furious with her, but to her surprise he said kindly to her, "Don't feel bad. You will make it all right, and one of these days you will be a Moses and go back south to lead and teach your people. Don't be discouraged, keep on trying, and you will make it alright." His kind words made her feel a little better; she just needed a little help to study. She knew she had to put in extra hours of study and keep up with the rest of the class. Her determination to do her best kept her going. That night she asked the dean if she could stay up a little longer to study. When the dean returned at midnight and saw her light still on, she knocked and asked why her light was on. Anna told her she was given permission to stay up, but did not think it would take all night. By two o'clock that morning Anna had finished her homework and was very happy the next day when she attended class.

Not only was Anna slow in her studies, but also in social activities. In fact, the girls at the school often referred to her as the "green girl from the South." One day as she walked by a group of girls they laughed and made jokes of the way she talked, repeating some of her country sayings. She would interrupt their joking and say, "Never mind, green things grow," and kept walking with her chin up. She was a little hurt, but she bit her lip and vowed to overcome all those odd things they were saying about her and show them some day that "green things will grow."

It was a beautiful sunny afternoon. The girls wanted to take a hike in the woods, but they were afraid to go. The Dean told them to ask Anna to go with them since she was familiar with the woods and was older, then they would have permission to go. When they asked Anna to go, she did not want to go at first because she needed the time to study, but she thought about it and decided to go. She always loved being in the woods in God's great outdoors. It was fun identifying all the plants and the trees. There were chestnut and apple trees throughout the woods and they were loaded with nuts and fruit. Being somewhat of a tomboy, she threw rocks at the chestnut tree to make the nuts fall to the ground, climbed apple trees and picked apples for the girls. The girls sat on the ground and enjoyed their nuts and fruit, thanking Anna for coming with them and showing them a good time. After that, she was not talked about anymore and the younger girls looked up to her.

The year at Mount Vernon was very hard for Anna because she did not attend elementary school. Everything she had learned to that point had been self-taught or through the private tutoring that Elder Dyo Chambers had given her. Here she was at Mount Vernon Academy, reaching toward the higher grades trying to be very diligent in her studies, worked very hard to keep up with the rest of the class, but it was still very challenging. Some of her classmates saw the predicament that she was in and had compassion for her. They formed study groups to help outside of school hours. By hard study and much prayer she made an "A" in all of her classes except one. She had demonstrated that "green things really grow."

As the school year came to a close, all of the other students were rejoicing because they were going home. Anna was not rejoicing, she loved school and she was not going back to her home and family in Mississippi, but instead returning to Chattanooga to stay with Brother and Sister Chambers. She was happy and excited to be back in the Chamber's home and wanted them to see how much she had learned in the year at Mt. Vernon Academy. The Chambers were pleased to see her and the change in the young lady that they had sent to school. She looked more confident and did not seem to be as timid as she was when she left for the Academy. Anna wished that her mother could see her; maybe she also would be proud of her daughter. Still she had not heard from her family in Mississippi, so she continued to write to let them know how she was doing.

The city of Chattanooga was chosen as the place to hold the first gathering of all the churches in the Southern Mission Field. It was called Camp meeting. Several leaders within the Southern Union traveled to Chattanooga months in advance to seek out a site and make preparations for the meeting. Everyone was very anxious and excited about this new mission field and the opportunity to share their faith. Time was set aside to encourage the leaders and members with inspiring messages and training. It was where they could get new guidance in giving Bible studies, literature and books to help them in their work in the mission field. It was a difficult task getting people organized to prepare the site. One of the most important positions to fill was the job of cooking the meals for the attendees and the workers. No one wanted that job. Since Chattanooga was the host city for the meeting and Anna was a charter member of the Chattanooga church, they asked her to do the job. She had never cooked for anyone but her family and even then it was just simple meals. The organizers felt that Anna was up to the task. After much persuasion, she thought that she would give it a try and cook for the forty people that were to attend the meeting. She had been a member of the church for two years and was willing to do anything to further the cause.

Two nurses from Battle Creek were among the attendees at the Chattanooga Camp meeting, Emma Washburn and Rosa Starr. They had just graduated from Battle Creek Sanitarium as self-supporting missionary nurses. Dr. John Harvey Kellogg sent them to attend the meetings and to teach classes about healthy living. In those days the Seventh-day Adventist strongly advocated that health reform was the right arm of the message and whenever possible, doctors and nurses were urged to locate in the cities where the message had not been preached. Since they were there to teach healthy living, Emma and Rosa helped Anna to plan healthy menus, and others helped in preparing the foods.

The kitchen tent was placed near the dining tent, the men made the tables and benches for the people to sit. The kitchen was not stocked; there were no cooking utensils and only a second-hand cooking stove. They borrowed pots and pans from members in the area who could spare them. Since Anna was the main cook, she stayed in a small tent close to the cooking area in order to be ready early in the morning to prepare the meals for the group. Anna was very nervous about this new venture. Being new to the faith, she wanted to work where she was needed most. She was very busy trying to get the dining tent and kitchen organized. The two nurses, Rosa and Emma developed healthy menus. Elder Sharp and his wife and daughter, Elder and Sister Chambers, encouraged and helped her to get everything started in preparing the meals. The meeting was larger than anyone had expected, instead of preparing to feed forty people three meals a day, it was over a hundred meals that needed to be prepared. The first few days were scary for Anna, on some days not enough food had been prepared, or it was not tasty enough, but Anna continued to cook the meals. The first Sabbath she prepared baked beans, the weather was hot and there was no refrigeration, so the beans did not keep very well. Several people became sick, but the nurses and doctors were there ready to look after them.

The meeting was for ten days with six meetings a day. Anna was only able to attend six meetings during the entire time. She felt that cooking the meals for the group, introducing them to healthful foods was a ministry. Elders G. I. Butler, R. M. Kilgore, G. W. Colcord, and Elder Smith Sharp and other workers were in attendance. This first camp meeting in Chattanooga marked a new day in the work of the Southland and brought courage and strength to the entire membership. The attendees were fed the spiritual food as well as the physical food; the latter might not have been as well received as the spiritual food. This was a job she would never forget! When the camp meeting was over, she was paid five dollars for her work. She was grateful for the money and the experience. She never cooked for a camp meeting again, and never again did she complain about anybody's cooking.

Battle Creek Sanitarium

Chapter 4

$\mathscr{A}$nother year had ended at Mt Vernon Academy and the students were returning home. Anna returned to the home of Elder and Mrs. Chambers in Chattanooga. Upon her arrival, Anna was surprised to find Elder Chambers in poor health. Concerned about the health of both of them, she knew that returning to Mount Vernon Academy for the next school term was going to be a problem. She began to think of how she could help the Chambers so they would not have to worry about how she was going to attend the next year of school. Anna too, was worried. She knew that she wanted to return to school but at the same time she did not want to be a burden to the Chambers. There was no need to write home to ask her mother for money because her mother did not want her to go to away to school, so she did the next best thing, she prayed. Somehow a door was going to open for her. God had not let her down yet in her journey to make a better life for herself. That evening after dinner, Mr. and Mrs. Chambers and Anna talked about how they were going to help her return to school in the fall.

A few weeks later, they received word that Dr. Paulson and his brothers were opening the industrial department of Battle Creek Sanitarium in Battle Creek Michigan. Anna remembered at camp meeting the past summer, the two nurses, Emma Washburn and Rosa Starr. They were from Battle Creek and they thought she should attend Battle Creek Sanitarium. The two young nurses wrote letters of introduction to the school on Anna's behalf. Elder Chambers wrote letters to Dr. John Harvey Kellogg and others he knew at Battle Creek telling them about Anna's situation and if there was anything they could do to help her. He also told them they would not be disappointed because she was a brave young lady from Mississippi seeking an education. By the time the school was to open, Anna received word that she was accepted in the Battle Creek Industrial School. Overjoyed and filled with numerous emotions it was very hard for her to sleep that night. Again she wrote her mother in Mississippi telling her that she would be attending school in Michigan. Even though she did not respond to her, she knew that she would be proud of her. If it were possible for the family to help her, they would.

Her friends in Chattanooga told her of the cold climate in Michigan as well as the coldness of the people. They said the people would be so busy that they would have little time to spend with a strange girl from the south. They cautioned Anna not to expect the warm hospitality in Michigan that she was accustomed to in the South. She listened to all they had to say, but deep down in her heart she had a made up her mind that she would go to the school and makes a point of being friendly to everyone. She vowed that before the year was over she would know everyone's name.

When she arrived at Battle Creek, she delivered the letters of introductions to Dr. Kellogg, Professor W Prescott, and Elder L A. Hoopes, and went back to her room to wait. Anna was not a girl who could just sit around and twiddle her thumbs doing nothing, so she decided to take a walk around the campus. Admiring all the buildings on the campus, with all the trees, she wondered how it would be in the winter when the trees lost their leaves and snow would cover the ground. She went in and out of several buildings but saw no one that she knew. She walked past the laundry and decided to go inside. There she found a girl from Mt. Vernon Academy who was ironing. She was happy to find a familiar face; she immediately began talking and asked if she could help with the ironing. There was a vacant board next to her, so Anna proceeded to iron and talk. For a while the room was silent, until one of the girls spoke.

"Here comes the manager. The new girl is going to get us into trouble." Anna was not listening and kept talking. The manager came to her and said:

"You are a new girl here, are you not?"

"Yes," Anna responded.

"Who sent you here?" he asked.

"No one, I just got tired of doing nothing, so I came up here and went to work." He smiled and went on his way. After he left, the other girls told her that they were not supposed to talk while working.

"Why didn't you tell me? I did not know the rules." After that incident, there was no more talking, and thankfully, no one was punished

On Sunday, all the new people who had not been assigned work were told to report to the "Annex," to Mrs. Hall, the industrial school matron, to receive their work assignments. When the matron had assigned all the girls work, there were two girls left, and Anna was one of them.

They waited for a while; all sorts of thoughts were running through Anna's mind. Suppose she could not get work, how was she going to stay at the school? All of a sudden the matron of the laundry came in excited.

"I need two girls for the laundry; two of my best girls were taken by Miss Aldrich for the cafeteria at the sanitarium!" Mrs. Hall replied, "There are only two new girls left, here they are, you may have them." New girls! I always get to take what is left," the matron said. Come on let me see what you can do."

Anna bit her lip to keep from saying what she felt, and followed Mrs. Hall to the laundry. She was glad because she had already had friends there, but, when she entered the laundry, her friend from Mount Vernon was the one who was transferred to the Cafeteria. The matron of the laundry was quite disturbed that she was given the new girls. She did not want to go through the process of training them on how to do the job. Anna was assigned to mop the floors and she finished her work well before the experienced helper. All of the tasks assigned to her that day were done very well and quickly. The matron apologized for doubting her working capabilities and was very pleased with her work. She was very happy, this was what she had wanted all her life....to be educated and trained and be "somebody." Her schedule was four hours in class and six hours working in the laundry. After a few days, Anna enrolled in the Industrial School. Her credits were checked from Mt. Vernon Academy and they found that she needed more preparatory work. Professor Bell taught the math and English classes and Mr. Hoover, who was the bookkeeper for the Sanitarium, taught the bookkeeping class. She worked for eight months completing all the requirements to enter the nurse's class. While working in the laundry, she made extra money ironing for the nurses and medical students. She gave the extra earned money to the matron, but she gave it back to her, and stated that she should keep the money. After about a year, Anna was able to pay her expenses in the Industrial School and had enough money to buy personal items.

The biggest problem for Anna was money to pay for the book. She did not want to write back to Brother Chambers and ask for more money, because they had already done so much for her. The only thing she could do was to ask the Lord. She continued to work in the laundry, doing anything she could to get extra work to buy her books. One day a letter came from Brother Chambers, she did not open it right away, thinking that they were writing to see how she was doing in school. When she finally opened the letter, to her surprise there was money in the envelope. His letter read, "Books cost money, use this to help buy them." This was the answer to her prayer. With the money she had saved, it was enough to buy the books needed for her classes. Now, she did not have to borrow books or study with someone else.

English and Bookkeeping classes were the largest. The teacher that was sent to teach the class was not from the Battle Creek College. She was a public school teacher who was taking advanced studies in nursing. The class was not very happy and became critical, and soon it was impossible for the teacher to settle the discussions in the class. The members of the class went to Dr. Kellogg with their grievances. He was very considerate and decided to secure a good teacher whom he was sure could teach the class. Someone asked, "Who is it?" "Must I give you the name now?" asked Dr. Kellogg. "Well, I'm going to try to get you the man who wrote the book. Will that do? "Oh Yes," the class shouted.

The next day the class met as usual with the same teacher. They were very unhappy and impatient with her. Finally, someone said, "Here he comes!" They all looked out the window and saw an old man with a long gray beard riding a bicycle. The wind was blowing, and his beard was spread out around his face, which made him look like Santa Claus. Soon the old gentlemen came into the classroom, he was introduced to the class and the day was spent getting acquainted. The students were very disappointed that so much time had been wasted. After all, they were working hard trying to pay for their education. Finally, the professor said, "I have revised the book that you currently have, and we will study out of the revised edition, Book III." "I cannot change! I have spent all my money buying books and I cannot buy another one," Anna said loudly. "Now I will take all the new books back and give you a copy of Book III, revised edition, in exchange. Is that fair?" Anna was so happy about the book exchange and most of all she was excited that the author of the Book III, Professor G. H. Bell was the teacher.

As mentioned before, Mr. Hoover the bookkeeper for the Battle Creek Sanitarium taught the bookkeeping class. It was not an easy class, one by one students dropped out until there were only two girls left and Anna was one of them. The young men in class teased the girls and said it would not be long before they dropped out of the class.

One day there was a long and difficult assignment. Mr. Hoover suggested that we take half of the assignment, but the young men laughed and said,

"No let's take it all in one lesson, we can do it."

The teacher looked at the two young ladies then said, "I am afraid it is too long for you." Anna was always a competitive person and loved a challenge.

"Give it to us. If the young men can do it we can too."

All right Mr. Hoover said, "Take it." The class was excused

That night Anna and her classmate Karen Mitchell asked the matron for permission to stay up late to study together. They worked and worked until two o'clock in the morning completing the assignment. Finally, it was finished and they were very satisfied and pleased with themselves. The next day they went to class trying not to show how satisfied they were that they had completed the assignment. After the roll was taken, Mr. Hoover then smiling said:

"Well, did you have any trouble getting through your lesson?"

"Yes," several of the young men shouted.

Only one young man had completed the assignment. Anna did not tell the class how long it took them to complete the assignment. They smiled at the young men and turned over their completed assignment.

There was an abundance of snow that year and Anna did not have enough warm clothing for the cold Michigan weather. Her room was in a cottage heated by a stove. Working in the laundry all day until ten o'clock at night and going out in the cold to return to her room in the cottage caused her to have a severe case of tonsillitis. During class she could hardly speak, all she could do was to listen to the other students. Although she was sick with a temperature of 104, it did not stop her from continuing to work in the laundry. One morning a nurse came in to pick up her laundry and noticed that Anna did not look well. The nurse was very surprised that she was working with the high temperature and immediately took her to the sanitarium to get medication to relieve the temperature. Instead, she ended up admitting her to the hospital. After two days of treatments, Anna felt so good that she checked out of the sanitarium and went back to work without their permission. As a result, she had a relapse and was confined to her room for thirty-six hours. The head nurse was very upset with her, and told her that anyone who did not know how to take care of themselves could not be admitted into the nurses' class. Anna was very upset, because she had worked hard, and so many people had helped her. She promised that nothing like that would ever happen again.

Accepted into the Nurses Class

At the end of the year, she had completed all the preparatory work with honors and was eligible for the nurses' class. Anna continued to work in the laundry until she received a notice to join the nurses' class which was being organized. When asked why she had not attended the Class before, Anna told the head nurse what she had said earlier about her not taking care of herself. The head nurse laughed and said, "I did not mean what I said, but only wanted to make you realize to take care of yourself."

Anna enrolled in the nurses' class finally. Her dream was coming true, and she was very happy and made a promise that she would do everything in her power to complete all the requirements. She wrote a letter to Elder and Mr. Chambers telling them the good news that she was accepted into the nurses' class. Excited, but still a little timid, she wondered if she could keep up with the rest of the students. She was never one to run away from a challenge and tackled her studies just as devotedly as she plowed the fields for her mother before she left home to get an education. Anna was concerned that she had not heard from her mother and the rest of her family in Mississippi. She continued to write even though they may not be able to read the letters. Someone there could read the letters so she would know how she was doing and that she was still in school. Home was always on her mind. She wondered how she was going to help her family back home when she completed her education. But for now, she had to concentrate on her studies and maybe by the time she finished, it would be clear to her what she was going to do with all the knowledge she learned at the Battle Creek Sanitarium. Each student in the class was given two nurses' uniforms, two pairs of shoes, and the required books for the first year's work. The students worked as nurses' aides while they were in training to become a professional nurse. This was considered nurses in training and no wages were paid. Each student was required to sign a statement that they desired to take the course for the purpose of becoming a missionary nurse and not a professional nurse to go out into the world to make money.

The first half of the year was spent as a helper in the strength-test room. Anna was the right person for this work because one of the requirements was the person had to have good writing skills. Anna's writing skills were excellent and remained until her death. The department found out that she could swim and assigned her to the swimming pool for six hours a day to teach the nurses and patients how to swim, she never told them how she learned to swim.

After the training period was over, Anna remained in the strength-test room because the department needed someone with her experience. She was given a list of patients to care for in the treatment rooms and was on-call for relief work. Just as she was getting a good start at real nursing training activities, the matron of the laundry became ill. The manager came to the treatment room and requested that Anna return to the laundry to help out until they could find someone else. Of course Anna hated to leave her position in the strength-test room, but she always went where she was needed the most. Upon her return to the laundry, she was amazed at the stack of clothes that had piled up. There was list after list of "specials" that needed to be taken care of. When she walked in, the rest of the students at the ironing room gave a sigh of relief, saying, "finally, we have someone who knows what they are doing." That made Anna feel better about leaving the nurses training class.

She tried to forget about the nurses' class and diligently assumed the work of matron of the laundry. For three weeks, working eighteen hours a day, taking two of her meals on the job, she worked tirelessly to get all the orders out and to get the laundry in order. The other ladies in the laundry were glad to work with Anna because she was organized. They wished that she would stay, but Anna had other plans. Word came to her that the matron of the laundry would not return. Anna was asked to stay on, but she informed the administration that she came to Battle Creek to be a nurse, and wanted to complete the classes that she started. They soon found someone to replace her in the laundry and she returned to her nursing class.

Anna returned to work in the treatment room, but unfortunately the patients were assigned to someone else. After a few weeks of working between the strength-test department and as a nurse's aide again, she could not secure a full-time case because of the hours spent in the strength-test department and swimming pool. Even though she was not happy with her assignment, she worked in whatever area that was assigned to her. In reviewing the hours needed for completion of the first year, Anna found out that because of her workload, she was short of the required hours needed to complete the semester, but, did not know how many hours until the final review. There was nothing that she could do, but to continue to work and pray that the Lord would work it out for her.

For some strange reason, Anna seemed to get all of the mentally ill patients. Each one was different but Anna managed to be patient with them as she tried to get them to trust her. One case in particular was a lady who was a maniac and very difficult to handle. One day the regular nurse had to be off longer than usual. The patient knew that Anna was new on the job. The lady was to go to the treatment room for her daily treatment. At first it was difficult for Anna to get the lady to the treatment room, but with the help of another nurse, Anna was able to get her to the room with the nurse in charge, while Anna stood guard at the door.

When the treatment was over it seemed as if the patient resented Anna being there and rushed toward her with great force and would have thrown her down, but Anna backed up against the wall and refused to move. When she saw that she could not push Anna away, she cried out, "You big old ox of a girl," and turned quickly and ran down the stairs to her room locking the door before Anna could get there. Anna was frightened because she did not know what might happen. She stood by the door listening for any unusual noises. Finally, an orderly came by and she sent him to get the master key so that the room could be opened. When Anna entered the room, the maniac was angry and again she attacked Anna. She backed up against the door and again refused to move. The lady pinched and slapped Anna a few times, but nurses are taught not to use force with patients. Anna just stood there and took it for a while. She remembered that the regular nurse told her if she could not calm the lady, to repeat Bible verses to her. Anna began repeating memory verses and to her surprise it worked, the lady calmed down and listened to her. Anna was exhausted from the day and was very glad when the regular nurse returned.

At the end of the year, the students were asked to give a report on the areas and hours they had worked. When Anna completed her report and the final review was completed, she was short one hundred hours. What was she to do? There was no way that she could make up the hours. With her report she attached a note:

> *"You can see how my work has been in several depart-*
> *ments, and the rest of the time I was held at the nurse's*
> *headquarters subject to call for relief work. I was al-*
> *ways faithful to my post of duty, but I do not have the*
> *required number of hours. I leave it with you, praying*
> *that the Lord will impress upon you what to do."*

After a few days she received a call from the head nurse to report to her office. The head nurse informed her that after reviewing her record for the year, the committee felt that she should not have to make up any time and that she was entitled to go on with the class. Once more the Lord had heard her prayers and worked in her behalf. She was promoted to the second year class with a salary and was able to buy her uniforms, books and other supplies. For once she did not have to worry about where the money would come from to continue her journey of becoming a missionary nurse. She wrote a letter home to her mother and the rest of the family, telling them of her experience and told them not to worry, her hard work was paying off.

The remaining years in the nurses' course were very challenging. The Training School of Battle Creek College was known as the American Medical Missionary College. Part of the time the medical students studied in Chicago and part-time in Battle Creek. On one occasion, the mission workers, while out canvassing and introducing health foods, came to a home where there was a very sick lady. The family at first would not let the mission workers into the house, but he asked to be allowed to come in and pray for the lady. Being Christians, they allowed him to come in. It was the home of Serapta M.I. Henry, national evangelist of the Women's Christian Temperance Union (WCTU). When the worker completed his prayer, he urged them to send their mother to the Battle Creek Sanitarium for treatment. The daughter was very impressed with what the mission worker was explaining to them about the treatments at the Sanitarium. He convinced the other family members to let her go.

Within a few days arrangements were made for Mrs. Serepta. M.I Henry to travel to Battle Creek Sanitarium for treatment. She boarded an express train and was taken to Battle Creek Sanitarium, in Battle Creek Michigan arriving on August 31, 1896, along with her daughter, doctor and minister. Upon her arrival, she was given special care and attention by the best doctors, Dr. John Harvey Kellogg himself, who carefully examined her. After several days of tests, Dr. Kellogg told the family that he could not cure her. She had a serious case of organic heart trouble, and nothing short of a miracle could help, but they could give her treatments which would make her last days easier. Of course, all were disappointed, but the decision was made to remain at the Sanitarium for a while. The staff at the Sanitarium did everything they could to make Mrs. Henry comfortable. One day when the chaplain came by to see her on his regular visit, she asked if she could be anointed and prayed for.

"You are all Christians. I am a Christian. Why can't I be healed?" she said.

The Chaplain responded by saying, "It is not up to me, it us up to God." The chaplain told the doctors about her request to be anointed. After discussions with the family, Mrs. Henry's request was granted. The time was set, the elders were called and the attending physician took Mrs. Henry to the chapel in a wheel chair. Notices were sent to all the nurse, department heads, and helpers, telling what was going to take place at a certain hour that day, and requesting everyone to unite in prayer for this sick patient. The prayers were answered and at the conclusion of the anointing service, Mrs. Henry walked back to her room. Of course, this was a glorious victory of faith! When she was examined again the next spring, there were no signs of the former heart problems.

Restored to her natural vigor, Mrs. Henry resumed her evangelistic duties and preached to an audience of twenty-five hundred in the Dime Tabernacle. Word quickly spread throughout the community about her miraculous healing. When the Women's Christian Temperance Society heard about Mrs. Henry being healed, all rejoiced greatly. She later studied and accepted the teachings of the Adventist Church, becoming an active lecturer and writer until her natural death some years later in 1900.

News came to the Sanitarium that there was a famine in India, and our own missionaries, some of whom were Battle Creek doctors and nurses were facing a shortage of food. Dr. Kellogg called all the doctors, nurses and students together and read the cablegram that he had received. He appealed to the staff to make a sacrifice of their food by going on a Hindu diet for one week. They were to cut out everything from their board bill except those things which the sanitarium would not have to buy. About five hundred students raised their hands to participate in this special diet. Special tables were arranged and at the end of the week $500 had been saved. The staff liked it so well that they decided to carry on and sacrifice another week. As a result of their plan, $1,000 in famine-relief funds was raised. Later when Anna went to India as a missionary, she saw how the people had suffered because of a lack of food. She was glad that she had a part in helping to raise funds for the famine-relief. During her work in India, Anna taught five of the orphan children who had been saved from starvation by our missionaries in Calcutta during that famine.

Returning to Mississippi

Chapter 5

After four years of training as a nurse at the Battle Creek Sanitarium, the time came for the students to decide what they were going to do with their learning experience. They had been trained to be missionary nurses and it was time to put their years of study to work. Dr. Kellogg called a meeting with the class and told them that another class was being formed and our class should go out into the mission fields and engage in self-supporting medical missionary work. There was a great need for medical missionaries in all parts of the world and in the United States. "Who will go?" Dr. Kellogg asked. Anna raised her hand. "I will go."

Anna had completed all of the requirements for graduation except for the practical training. This is why she volunteered to do medical missionary work. It would allow her to complete the practice needed for graduation. The volunteers were interviewed by a committee to receive instructions, equipment and supplies for their assignments. When Anna was called for her interview, Dr. Kellogg asked her what she wanted to do and where she wanted to work. She stood up and firmly announced that she wanted to return home in Mississippi. He was surprised but pleased. "Fine, few people would want to do that. Provide me and the committee with your plan at our next meeting," he said. What could be a more fertile mission field than her hometown of Six Town? During

Anna's years at Battle Creek, she had sent pictures home to her family. It was hard for them to imagine that a place like Battle Creek existed.

A few weeks after the interview, Anna presented Dr. Kellogg and the Committee with her plan for starting the school in her home state of Mississippi. To her surprise she was advised that the medical missionary society would take care of the transportation costs back home. This time Anna was happy packing her suitcase, and most of all her nurse's uniform that she had sacrificed and worked so hard to wear.

The day finally arrived for Anna to leave Battle Creek Sanitarium. She was told to go to the office to receive her instructions. Dr. Kellogg handed her a voucher for travel from Battle Creek, Michigan to Cincinnati, Ohio and $20.00 for incidental expense. She was also given a letter to give to the ticket agent advising them to give her the missionary rate for purchasing her ticket. She was given another letter to the Review and Herald Publishing House stating that she could get as many of Dr. Kellogg's *Number One Physiology Books* as she needed. The books were going to be a great help in teaching the students at the school she was going to start. Anna left Battle Creek feeling very pleased. She had worked and studied for six years to get an education. Now she was ready to go out into the mission to put all her training to work. What a better place to start than her home in Mississippi

On the way home, she stopped in Chattanooga to visit with the Chambers, the family that she stayed with when she first left Mississippi. She was very sad to learn that Mr. Chambers died while she was away in school. Mrs. Chambers was glad to see Anna and impressed with how she had matured into a well-rounded young lady. A great improvement from the young girl from Mississippi who she first met a few years ago. That evening, they stayed up and talked about her experiences throughout her school years and how she appreciated their support and guidance. Mrs. Chambers told Anna that if she passed away before the Lord came, that her work would continue through Anna, which made Anna feel proud. She promised that she would work for the Lord the rest of her life. It was a short but sweet visit. Anna left Mrs. Chambers the next day and made her way home to Mississippi.

On the train home, she wondered how life was going to be upon her return. Would her mother welcome her? How would the community accept her? Would they think that she was better than everyone, because she had gone away to school? All of these thoughts ran through her mind as the train made its way to Ellisville, Mississippi. Finally, the train pulled into the station. When she made it to the platform, she saw Howard her brother, waiting for her with the ox wagon. All of the questions that she had in her mind went away when she saw the big smile on his face.

The trip from Ellisville to Six Town was about twenty miles and took all day. It was a good time for Howard to bring her up to date on what was going on at home and in the community. Anna and Howard always confided in each other about their personal feelings. He was so proud of his sister. He was overjoyed to have his sister back home and excited that they were finally going to go to school. She enjoyed looking at the freshly planted fields and the tall pine trees as the ox wagon slowly moved across the bumpy and dusty road.

When they arrived at her mother's house, all of the relatives in the community were there to greet her. Her mother had cooked a big dinner and spread out on a long table with a white tablecloth. Relatives brought food and they had a good time welcoming Anna back home. They had forgotten about her new faith and were eager to hear about her experiences while she was away at school. So, after dinner she entertained them by telling the stories about her years at Battle Creek Sanitarium. Anna was wondering how she was going to tell them about her plans to start a school. This would have been the first school in the community. She asked if anyone had gone to school since she left. The answer was no, because they were the children of Newton Knight and of mixed heritage, they were not allowed to attend any of the schools in the area.

While she had a captive audience, she showed them books and the charts that Dr. Kellogg had given her and put on her nurse's outfit. She stood in the midst of the group and told them, "Now all of this is to be used for the good of you and your children and all the people in the area, if you will only co-operate in the work. We must work together and thereby banish darkness and superstitions from our midst by letting the light of Christian education come in." They were very excited about the new school and were eager to help in any way they could.

Finding a building suitable for a school was very hard to do. Her uncle had an old log cabin that was vacant and he told her she could use it for the school. The cabin had a fairly good roof, a partial chimney and a fireplace. Everyone pitched in to help turn the old log cabin into a schoolhouse. They patched up the cracks and cut down trees to make benches for the children to sit on. There was only one window, so she placed her desk and chair near it. By the time school was opened that winter, the one room schoolhouse was ready to receive the children. On the first day of school, Anna rang the school bell and the students came running with big smiles on their faces, all dressed in their best clothes. The school opened with twelve students, all of her relatives, both children and adults. Those who attended the school really enjoyed the classes taught by Anna, and seldom missed a day. When it was cold, Anna and the children gathered wood and pine knots to be used to make a fire in the fireplace which was their only source of heat. The benches that the children sat on were placed in the middle of the room near the fireplace. The children took turns sitting on the front bench to keep warm. The one room schoolhouse did not have enough light for the children to study their lessons. Pine knots were placed on the fire which provided a glow of light for the children to see. It was unusual to snow in Mississippi, but on one particular day is snowed, so a big fire was made in the fireplace. Not long after, the partial chimney which was made of sticks and clay fell, and set the school on fire. However, they caught it in time and put the fire out by throwing snowballs. This was a scary situation for everyone. The chimney was rebuilt, but this time with much safer materials.

The families did not have much money. It was very hard to pay the one dollar a month tuition fee. Most of the children and the families did odd jobs at the school such as cutting wood, cleaning the school, and keeping the ground clear of brush to defray the tuition cost. They were paid five cents an hour for their work which went toward their tuition fee. Even though Anna had gone away to school for six years, she still had her four acres of land that was planted in cotton. When the time came to harvest the cotton, all the students helped to pick the cotton and the money received from the sale was used to pay the expenses and help the children with their tuition. Her father Newton stopped in on occasion to see how the school was doing. He was very proud of what his daughter was teaching the students and even contributed to the expenses of the school.

During the summer of her first year of school, she received a letter from Dr. Kellogg of Battle Creek Sanitarium asking her and a few other students who had started missionary work, to return to the Sanitarium and complete a postgraduate course. While taking the class, extra help was needed to care for a large number of patients who were there that summer. Anna knew this was a perfect opportunity to earn extra money for her school, so she stayed and worked the summer. After completing the postgraduate course, she returned to Mississippi to continue her school in Gitano.

Anna was always a woman with a vision. She had plans to build a new school, a larger one that did not have any cracks in the walls or floor. She had sketched a plan and already started clearing the land. She was building the new school on part of the forty acres her mother had given her to build a home. Without money she could not start the new school, so they continued to use the old log cabin. Another cotton harvest in the fall, and there would be enough money from the sale of the cotton to start the new schoolhouse.

After about a year and a half of teaching in her mission school, she received a letter from her classmate Julia Luccock who was taking care of a patient in Alabama. She stated that she wanted to visit Anna for a few days. By the time the letter reached Anna, Julia was on her way to Six Town. Anna had never talked about her family with her friends while away at school. They did not know that her father was white and her mother was half white. No one knew about the kind of house they lived in or anything about the community she lived in. Anna was nervous about her coming to visit, but she was already on her way.

Anna could not go to the train station in Ellisville to meet Julia, because she was teaching school. She tried to get her uncle to go to meet Julia, but he said he could not meet a strange woman from the north since he had no idea how to approach her. Finally, she was able to get her faithful brother Howard and a cousin to go with the horse and wagon to Ellisville to meet Julia. Anna showed them Julia's picture, gave them a dollar a piece to pick her up and bring her back to the house. Anna told them that Julia would wait for them in front of the Alice hotel in Ellisville. They went to Ellisville, but did not have the courage to go to the hotel to meet Julia. Half the day had passed when Julia saw Howard and his cousin standing around. It occurred to her that they were there to pick her up. She approached them:

"I am Julia, are you here to pick me up?"

Yes ma'am," Howard said.

The ride back to Six town was a long and quiet one. Julia tried to start a conversation but with only yes and no as answers.

Anna was so glad to see Julia; they stayed up most nights just talking about all the plans for the future. Both of them told about their experiences after leaving Battle Creek Sanitarium. Anna was so thrilled to have her visit that she forgot about her living conditions. Julia did not seem to mind at all. Her father Newt stopped by to see how things were going, but he never talked much. He was always sitting on the porch deep in thought. Julia was very intrigued by him, but never asked any questions.

Anna shared with Julia her plan to build a new school. She showed her the rough sketch that she had drawn. Julia was very interested in what Anna was trying to do. She looked over the plans and made a few changes. Soon the time came for Julia's visit to end. Anna was very sad but she knew that Julia was on her way to visit her family, and they were going to attend camp meeting in Iowa. When she left, she took the rough sketch of the plans for the school that she and Anna had talked about to show her father who was a builder. A few weeks later, Anna received the plans in the mail along with fifty dollars that Julia had solicited for the construction of the school. Anna was very grateful for this contribution and immediately started to work on building the school using the new plans.

As was the custom in the area, when anyone started a building project, the whole community came out to help. The older ladies prepared a wonderful meal with food that was freshly picked from the gardens. The men cut timber for the lumber, the women and children picked cotton on Anna's four acres and sold it and used the money for the building fund. After eight weeks of hard labor and united effort, the school was finally finished. It was the nicest school in the community and the surrounding area. People heard about it and came as far as seventy-five miles away to see the new school. It was a joyous time for everyone.

It was a bright sunny morning on the first day in the new school. Twenty-four excited students were there ready to begin classes in their new school. Anna's mother Georgeann stood in the school yard watching the children rushing to their new school. She remembered how Anna loved to teach play school when she was a child. Now she could see her daughter's dream fulfilled as a real educated teacher. The community was excited about the school because the children would have the opportunity to learn to read and write just like any other child in the area. They would not be left in the dark again when it came to learning just because they were considered the "white negroes," or part of the Newt Knight Klan. This was their school and they could not be turned away because of their mixed heritage. The school was named the Gitano School, because it was located near the Gitano community.

Not only did Anna teach school in her community, she also organized and taught two Sunday schools, six miles apart. One was a school for the adults, and then she would walk six miles to the black Baptist church in Soso where there were fifty to sixty people attending the classes in the afternoon. She wrote to the Graysville School in Tennessee and asked if they had any books they could send to her. They had heard about the missionary work that Anna was doing in her home state and gladly sent her books. With the books that Dr. Kellogg had given her and the *"Little Friend,"* a booklet for the children, she was able to carry on classes.

After Sunday school was over, classes in healthful cooking, canning, and how to preserve food were taught mainly to the adults. Because of the training that Anna had received from Battle Creek Sanitarium, she knew that they had to be taught about taking care of their bodies and eating healthy foods. The people were learning and accepting so many new things, but, it was hard to get them to turn away from all of the drinking and dancing. She had to work and pray hard about that, hoping that God would somehow change their hearts.

While Anna was away, different religious groups had moved into the area; one was a group of Mormons. They had heard about this woman who came back and was stirring up a lot of trouble and felt threatened by her. The Mormon preacher said a woman was not supposed to preach. They became angry with her especially when she taught against polygamy. They told a group of the most evil white folk in the county to try and stop her teaching. Word was sent to Anna that if she did not stop, they would wait for her on the road and kill her. She sent word back, "Just because I went away to school, it does not mean that I have forgotten how to shoot. When they are ready, I will be ready." Their threats did not scare Anna, because she knew the woods very well and always walked a different way on her way to and from the Baptist Church. She carried her revolver in her Bible case beside the *"Little Friend."* This went on for about a year finally the Mormons gave up and left the area.

Moonshiners were another group that lived in the area who were very upset with Anna. They had a very profitable business making and selling illicit liquor to the people who lived in the community. They would say things like, "This here woman has gone up North and got all these Northern ideas, and is bringing all this in here and getting these people stuck up, and trying to preach, going from one place to another holding meetings, there and here, we will fix her."

They sent word they would kill her and burn the school. While the words disturbed Anna, she continued on her mission.

Trying to be very careful and to keep the "moonshiners" off guard, she continued the practice of never traveling the same way.

But soon the men caught on to what she was doing. One Sunday, they were waiting for her. She was on horseback riding through the fields and then came back to the public highway. There were eight to ten white men, drunk waiting for her at the edge of the woods. There was a long stretch of road, about two miles, lined with pine trees on both sides. There in the woods she heard the men talking loud, shooting their guns and looking for Anna. On that particular day, she did not have her revolver. She had gotten religious enough to leave it at home. She continued her ride and just prayed a little prayer that the Lord would get her past these men without being harmed. Some of the men came down the road, meeting her, and the others were in back as if to surround her. Anna continued to ride her horse, "Red" in even strides looking them straight in the eyes.

"Good morning beautiful day," she said to the men.

The ones in the back began to move closer to her; soon she was surrounded by the men. By this time there was only one thing for her to do, she had to make a run for it. She leaned down and whispered in "Red's" ear and said, "Let's go." She dropped the reins, threw up her hands and slapped the horse on the side, which was the signal for him to run at high speed. She held on tight leaned over to the side to urge the horse to run faster. Red knew exactly what to do and ran through the mob of men so fast they did not know what was happening. The men were surprised, yelling and shooting their pistols, but neither the horse nor Anna was harmed. When she was at a safe distance, she patted "Red" and the horse slowed down to a trot. She thanked the Lord that "Red" had not forgotten the tricks she had taught him. When she reached home, she put the horse in the barn, gave him food and water and went into the house as if nothing ever happened.

On one occasion students were waiting for her in the schoolhouse. As soon as the class started, the door opened and three men walked in and took a seat in the back. Anna recognized them as some of the men that she had met on the road home and knew that they were there to cause trouble. As she began teaching the class, one of the men spat on the floor (Anna had a rule that no one was to spit on the floor). She stopped the class and said, "I thought I heard someone spit on the floor. If so, please don't do it again. If I am not correct, I beg your pardon." This certainly was not what the men expected, so they left the schoolhouse. Anna watched as they left to see which way they were going. The men dispersed into the woods, but instead of mounting their horses and leaving the area, they lingered around outside. Anna knew that there was going to be trouble. Anna hurriedly finished the class and dismissed the women and children. She and two of her older cousins remained behind to tidy up the schoolhouse and to make sure that the men did not come back to cause trouble. They could hear the men in the woods drinking and talking loud, they looked out the window and saw them coming toward the school. Finding the school closed, they were very upset. They started cussing and kicking the dirt in the ground. What they were not expecting was Anna and the Knight boys waiting for them. They soon found that the two "Knights" were too much for the three of them and they finally gave up and left the school yard. After that, Anna had different folks watch out for the school at night and to escort her back and forth to the schools.

The school year had ended and the children were already in the fields helping to plant the crops. Anna started her planting for the year and was preparing for the Mississippi hot summer. She was very pleased with her work in starting the school for her family. The parents of the children were very proud that their children had a school of their own. By now the moonshiners and the Mormons gave up on stopping Anna from teaching and did not bother her anymore. The school was the shining light in a community which had been darkened by superstition, racism and poverty. The enrollment remained constant at the school at year end. There were twenty-two students in the Gitano School, and the Sunday school in Soso had one hundred students.

At the end of the school year she was invited to teach at the Graysville School in Tennessee, the same school that she was turned away from a few years before because of her race. Anna was to teach First Aid classes to the Colporteurs and other students at the Summer Institute. This extra teaching duty gave her the opportunity to tell others about the work she was doing as a Self- Supporting Missionary even if it was in her own home state of Mississippi. This assignment allowed her to earn extra needed funds for the school. She held no grudges against the people there. The best revenge was that the young lady that they had turned away for her race was now standing before them as their teacher.

Mission Field of India

Chapter 6

*I*t was in May, 1901 a letter came from Dr. J. H. Kellogg of Battle Creek Sanitarium, inviting graduates who were involved in self- supporting work of Medical Missionaries to attend the General Conference Session as a delegate. The General Conference Session is a meeting of all the churches and conferences in the world of the Seventh-day Adventist Church. Dr. Kellogg had pushed for more exposure of the Medical Missionaries and the wonderful work they were doing after training at Battle Creek Sanitarium. Anna was excited to be one of the delegates attending the General Conference Session. She had never seen so many Christian people gathered and worshiping in one place in all her life. Each delegate invited by Dr. Kellogg was asked to give a report of their work after graduating from Battle Creek Sanitarium. When it came time for her to give her report, she stood proudly with her head held high and voice so clear, and stated her accomplishments after graduation. She talked about how she started and built a schoolhouse free of debt with twenty-four students, organized two Sunday schools in two different communities, and gave scores of lectures on health and temperance and first aid to the sick. After making her report, other delegates seemed to be impressed that a person fresh out of school could do so much with little funds.

Listening to several missionaries who had just returned from different countries around the world telling their experiences and the need of the area for trained nurses and teachers really touched Anna. There was one couple in particular Elder and Mrs., J. L. Shaw who had just returned from Africa and had been called to India. The Shaw's expressed a need for two trained nurses to go with them to help in Sanitarium in Calcutta. Immediately Anna thought about her wish to go to a foreign land to teach people about health and temperance. One day she overheard a group of nurses talking about the Sanitarium in Calcutta and the need for trained nurses. On impulse she said, "If they will send a man or women to take over my school in Mississippi, I will go to India." The word got to the committee and to her surprise she was called in for an interview. After several more interviews, Anna began to seek the advice of her friends as to whether she should go to India or return to Mississippi to continue teaching at her school. She found out quickly that this truly was a decision that she and the Lord would have to make. One of her classmates Donna Humphrey had also been asked to go, she too was undecided. There was only one thing for both of them to do, which was to go to the Lord in prayer. Anna returned to her room and prayed for answers. In her usual direct manner she prayed. "Lord, you know all things, and all needs, the work is all Thine. The people are Thine in Mississippi, India, and in the entire world. Lord, if You need me in India more than Mississippi, then take away this sorrow out of my heart and stop me from crying about it. If the sorrow and crying is taken away, then I'll know You are calling me to go to India.

Before she had finished her prayer, the tears stopped, she was at peace, and she had her answer. The next problem to be solved was who could take over the school in Mississippi. She remembered her friend Julia who had just got married, and had recently visited her in Mississippi and thought she and her husband could carry on the work at the school. She wrote a letter to Julia telling her about her decision to go to India, and asked if she and her husband would be willing to go to Mississippi and teach at the school. They could stay at her farm and use the land and everything as though it were theirs. A few weeks later she heard from Julia and they agreed to go to Mississippi. Arrangements were made for Julia and her husband to travel to Mississippi to teach at the school in Gitano. Anna wrote a letter to her mother telling her of her decision to go to India as a Missionary and that Mr. and Mrs. Atwood were going to take over the teaching at the school. She also told her mother to please allow them to stay at her home and make them welcome in the community. Anna did not return home to say good bye to her family or the students. She felt confident that she was leaving the school in good hands with Julia Atwood and her husband.

All arrangements had been made and Anna was ready to go to India as a Missionary Nurse in a foreign country that she knew nothing about. She and a few others joined the group going to India and boarded the train bound for New York. There were hundreds of people at the train station to see them off. It was such a thrilling experience, still she did not cry. Her heart was light because she knew that she was doing what the Lord had planned for her. Donna Humphrey, her classmate, also made the decision to go. Anna was glad that she had someone that she knew traveling with her on this journey.

After spending a few days in New York to get all the proper papers in order they sailed May 26, 1901. Traveling with the group was Elder and Mrs. J. L Shaw, Elder G K. Owen and her classmate, Donna Humphrey. For sixteen days and nights they never saw land, just the crystal blue ocean for miles and miles. She and her friend Donna often watched from the deck of the ship to see the fish as they gracefully jumped out of the water.

Watching the sunset over the rolling waves in the evenings was so beautiful. Finally, the ship pulled into port in Liverpool, England on Tuesday, June 6th. The next morning they boarded the train to London, England traveling across the English Channel and continued on by train through France. They took another smaller boat to sail down the Mediterranean, passing some of the islands she had read about in the Bible. When they came upon the Red Sea, she imagined the waters dividing and the children of Israel crossing over, and the Pharaoh's army being swallowed up by the huge waves. After thirty days of traveling by sea and land, the young Missionaries reached their destination, Bombay, India on Friday evening, June 26, 1901. Unfortunately they could not go ashore until the morning. The sun was shining bright but it looked as if it was a new sun, because she was in a different part of the world. Anna just stood on the deck of the boat and looked in amazement at the wonderful new world. She did not know what lay ahead of her, but she knew that there was work to be done and being a woman of determination, she was ready for it.

When they were able to leave the ship, the group could hardly make their way to Victoria train station because there were so many people. The streets were crowded with beggars and lepers in all stages lying along the streets. Suddenly the scene was not so beautiful anymore. Silently, she prayed that God would help her to help these poor people in some way. After arriving at the train station and waiting for the train to Calcutta, they realized that they needed to have food for the trip. A few members of the group decided to go and find food for lunch and missed the train. However, they were able to catch a later train to Calcutta. They were happy that everyone made it safely back together again and there was food and drink for their travels.

Traveling by train in India was a rough journey, and after thirty-six hours of traveling, the group reached the Howrah train station in Calcutta. Practically the whole mission family was at the train station to welcome them, but all they wanted to do was to get a good hot meal, take a bath and sleep for a while. After a few days of settling into her new surroundings, Anna had a chance to visit the city of Calcutta. She was surprised to find that it was a modern and beautiful city. It did not take her long to realize that all the things she had heard about were all too real; the poverty and the people who had not heard about the Truth. There was a lot of work to be done and so few people to accomplish the work.

Anna talked with the people who were already working in the sanitarium to find out what area needed the most help. She first started to work in the sanitarium in Calcutta as a nurse. Word came that someone was needed to go to the mission station in Karmatar about one hundred and sixty-five miles away. This mission school was opened in 1902 as a boarding school for European and Anglo-Indian children. Thekla Black and Anna Orr were the matrons of the school. One of the workers, Mr. Quantock, had taken ill and was not able to continue working at the mission, so he returned to the United States to receive medical care. Samantha Whities was in charge of the medical work and requested help. Anna was a trained nurse and capable of doing all types of work. Ms. Whities asked her to work at the Karmatar Mission School. Anna worked in various positions, from attending to the health needs of the students and the people in the village, to bookkeeping and teaching Bible and English. She was very busy with her work and enjoying helping the people. The village people were grateful for the medical help that the Karmatar Mission provided for them.

After working for a few weeks, Anna had a chance to look over the school grounds and wondered why there was not a vegetable garden. After all, healthy eating was one of main principles of the school. She was informed that they had tried for some time to have a vegetable garden but nothing would grow in the soil. But,

Anna grew up on a farm and she knew how to plant a garden. She took her hoe and showed the coolies how to prepare the soil. They balked at her and said that it will not work and nothing would grow. The coolies told her that she was wasting her time. Anna instructed the coolies to take a bullock cart and go to the river, fill gunny sacks with sand, mix it with the soil. Then mix in barnyard manure and add that to the mix. Anna remembered seeing an American plow in the yard and told the coolie to bring it to the garden area. The coolie protested and said she was mad and she did not know what she was doing and this kind of gardening will not work in India. Anna was a woman of determination and wanted to prove that it could be done. She had the coolies to hitch two bullocks to the turn plow and walk beside them to make them pull the plow. The ground was very hard but she managed to make good rows. She planted sweet potato slips in the top of the rows. Anna worked so hard and was wet with perspiration. It began to rain before the planting was complete and she was soaking wet. But, she had to finish the garden. She was told that if one wanted to retain their leadership with the natives, they must not fail in what they undertook.

Anna completed the gardening for the day and went to her bungalow, took a bath, ate dinner and then all went blank---- she fainted, for thirty-six hours she was unconscious. The native helpers were very frightened and at first did not know what to do. Samantha Whities had left for Calcutta by train that morning to get the monthly supplies and the helpers were the only ones there. They sent a telegram to Calcutta for Ms. Whities explaining Anna's condition, and for her to come back immediately. She was a little confused by the telegram and sent another nurse back to Karmatar to see what was going on. After a few days Anna regained consciousness. Although weak, she managed to sit in a chair to direct the coolies how to plant the remainder of the garden. The garden was planted with turnips, cauliflower, tomatoes, beets and other vegetables. The garden produced a harvest of vegetables that Karmatar had never seen before. The news spread quickly in the village that the Missionary really did make the American plow work wonders.

The Karmatar mission school had a very active printing press. The *Oriental Watchmen* and the *London Good Health* were printed twice a month. There were so many magazines that had to be mailed; the local post office could not handle it. Often times they had to bag and stamp the magazines individually, place them in large bags, and take the night train to Calcutta in order to mail them to the subscribers.

It was the summer of 1902, work was slow at the sanitarium in Calcutta and the school was out for the summer. A number of the workers were sent to canvas the neighborhood selling the periodicals. After careful consideration it was decided that Anna and Donna Humphrey, another nurse at the sanitarium, would go to sell the magazines to the English-speaking people. They also conducted classes on healthful eating wherever possible. This was a good way to introduce the community to the Calcutta Sanitarium and also to tell them about the food factory. Anna and Donna Humphrey, the young worker who traveled to India with Anna, set out on the journey to Allahabad to sell the magazines. They spent six weeks working in the city of Allahabad under the auspices of the Young Women's Christian Association (YWCA) to conduct health seminars which were very popular with the European population. The summers were very hot in Allahabad especially since they spent most of their time in the hot summer heat. Someone told them that it would be best to go to Simla, which was a mountain city, and that the weather would be cooler. On April 21, 1902 Anna and Donna started on their journey to the mountain city of Simla. When they arrived at the train station, they saw a friend who was the secretary of the YWCA of Allahabad. They told her they were going to the mountain city to finish out the summer and would return when it was cooler weather. Their friend said that she was very sorry to see them leave because they were doing such wonderful work. She asked if they had made reservations for Simla. "No," Anna replied. They were told that Simla was a popular area where people vacationed in the summer. Reservations needed to be made six months ahead of time in order to get a room. Now, Anna and Donna were worried. They had given up their room and their luggage was at the railway station. Their friend could see the trouble they were in. She gave them a letter and said: "When you get to Simla, take this letter to the YWCA, secretary at Valentine Cottage. If possible she will provide you with lodging for a few days until you can find a place. We have a holiday home there."

Anna thanked her for the letter and proceeded to buy the tickets for Simla. After they purchased two tickets to Simla, they found out that the train did not go directly to Simla; instead they had to travel to the city of Kalka which was fifty-eight miles from Simla. From Kalka they traveled by a tonga, which was a crude cart drawn by two horses. Arriving at Kalka, Anna and Donna made their way to the tonga station to secure their seats for the ride to Simla. Again, they were met with the same questions, "Did you make reservations?"

"No," Anna replied. "I am a stranger to the area and did not realize seats had to be reserved." The tonga driver fussed at her but Anna just stood there and smiled. Just then he was handed a telegram, telling him to sell two the seats because the people who originally purchased them were detained and would not arrive until the next day. The Lord had intervened for them again.

The ride to Simla was a rough and bumpy, but Anna did not mind, it reminded her of the ox wagon back home in Mississippi.

They were so thankful that they were able to get the seats on the tonga. They also had to be alert and make sure that they got off at the right place. The driver tried to put them off at one of the stops, the Chara Miadon, but Anna refused to get off. They did not speak the same language yet, she made him understand her. After making another stop, Anna sent Donna Humphrey up the hill to see if the Valentine Cottage was there. A few minutes later she came back smiling saying this was the right stop. The driver hurriedly took their luggage off the tonga and proceeded on his way with his mail delivery.

They made their way to Valentine Cottage and were glad to find the secretary at home. They handed her the letter and she said, "For some reason I could not leave the cottage when I was supposed to, now I know why." She informed Anna and Donna that they could only stay at the cottage for three days, because missionaries from Bombay had reserved the rooms. They all marveled at the way the Lord was providing for them. It was on a Friday afternoon when Anna and Donna settled into their rooms and prepared for the Sabbath. That evening at worship, they prayed to God to help them find suitable housing for the summer so they could carry on their work assigned to them.

The next morning after breakfast, they decided to spend the day on the mountainside to study their Sabbath School lesson. Later they planned to go into the village to find the lady they had met in Calcutta to solicit her help in finding a place to stay for the summer. Anna and Donna enjoyed their time looking out on the beautiful mountain and enjoying the cool weather. They decided to explore a little more to see if there was a park nearby. Just then a family of black monkeys surrounded them and chattered at them incessantly. Finally, they went on their way. Just as Anna and Donna started to walk down the hill, they saw a lady coming toward them. As she came nearer, they realized it was the lady they had been praying to find. They were both surprised to see each other.

"How did you get here? I usually go the longer way back, but for some reason, I decided to take this way home this time." Anna told her how they had prayed to find her, and needed help in finding a place to live. She told them of a little cottage that she had lived in before. We should pass by it on the way back to the Valentine Cottage. When Anna and Donna saw it, it was the perfect place and they really wanted the Cottage. On Sunday morning, their friend took them to meet the owner and to see if it was available for the summer. The owner said it was leased, but she had a large room in the main house we could have. Anna was very disappointed.

"No, we really would rather have the cottage since we will be staying the summer," Anna responded. While they were talking to her, a messenger again delivered a telegram. She read it and looked at them. Well ladies, somebody is looking out for you," the owner said. "The people who leased the cottage have decided to go to Darjeeling instead of Simla, and they ask me to sublease it, so you can have it."

Anna and Donna went back to the Valentine Cottage to gather their luggage and thanked the owner for allowing them to stay the few days. It was hard for everyone to believe how the Lord was continuing to work miracles for them. Truly, this was the place they were meant to be. Early Monday morning they moved into their cottage and remained there all season. The Lord blessed their work that summer. Donna Humphrey provided massages and health treatments to the upper-class folk while Anna spent her time with the village people. Through their efforts many books were sold and placed in the homes of the people, and the health seminars were very successful at the YWCA as it was in Calcutta. At the end of the summer they went down to Delhi, in the North

West Province of India, which was the winter headquarters of the lieutenant Governor of the Punjab. Donna Humphrey worked as a private nurse for lady Rivaz, wife of the Lieutenant Governor. Anna continued with her missionary work of selling books and magazines to the people in the village. They stayed there for two months before returning to Calcutta to continue the work at the Sanitarium.

One afternoon everyone seemed to be very upset. Anna did not know what was going on. She went to the matron of the Sanitarium to inquire about all the commotion. That was when she learned that her dear friend and co-worker Donna Humphrey died suddenly. It was March 4, 1903. Anna was heartbroken. Donna was a dear friend who had accompanied her on her first missionary tour. It was suggested to Anna that she may want to return home, but she instead decided to continue her work in India. She asked the Missions Committee to let her go back to Simla to complete the work started there the summer before. While waiting for the decision, she returned to Karmatar Mission to work there for a while.

Bad news just kept coming. Anna received a letter from home telling her that Mr. & Mrs. Atwood had to leave the school in Mississippi because of continued threats and violence from the same group of people who Anna had trouble with before. They did not feel safe living or working under those conditions and decided to leave. Anna was heartbroken that all the work she had put into the missionary project had gone up in smoke. Again she questioned herself and wondered why she was in India when her people needed her. She wrote to the General Conference and the local Conference asking if they could send someone to the school to continue the work. A letter was also sent to the people in the community stating that she had not been in India long enough to get a furlough to come home, but as soon as she was eligible, she would return to rebuild the school and continue the work. She asked them to have patience and faith in God, for surely some provision would be made. After she felt that she had done all she could to comfort her people in Mississippi, she returned to her missionary work in India. She continued the work that she and Donna Humphrey started, but was worried about the school in Mississippi. The children had waited so long for a school and now it was gone.

On April 15, 1903 at 9:30 P.M., Anna boarded the Eastern Indian Railway Express and traveled back to Simla. Later, Helen Wilcox joined her and together they worked for three years selling literature, conducting Bible studies and medical work as needed. Their mission was to work and do what was needed for the people of India. She had to pray earnestly that God would help her to make the right decision concerning the missionary work she had started at home in Mississippi. She continued to write letters to the Conferences urging them to send someone to teach at the school in Gitano, but she did not receive an answer. She knew that this was something she had to complete.

Chapter 7

Working at the Karmatar Mission, Anna worked in several positions such as business manager, English teacher, and assistant to the nurse in charge of the dispensary. There was little time for anything else. It seemed that every day was a new experience. On one particular day a group of natives riding in a bullock cart came to the Mission and earnestly asked if someone could come to their village to see a very sick woman. They said that all of the other witch doctors and faith healers had failed in their treatment of her illness, and she had been sick for month.

We knew if they came with a bullock cart, that it must be some miles away to the village. The head nurse, Miss Whities, asked Anna to go with her. They quickly gathered a few medical supplies and a clean jug of water to take with them. They also took one of the boys from the Mission to go along to interpret. Miss Whites rode on her bicycle ahead of Anna and the rest of the group. Soon she saw Miss Whites coming back stating that the lady was sick with a bad case of typhoid malaria fever and more supplies were needed. She told Anna and the young boy to go ahead and do what they could until she returned with the additional supplies.

They eventually reached the village and found that the sick woman was lying on a cot of woven coarse rice-straw ropes, no sheets or blanket, just a small cloth covering her body. Her body was frail, and they thought that she was already dead. The hut was filled with smoke from a charcoal bucket in which the natives had built a fire of dry cow dung to place under the cot of the poor woman to keep her warm. As a result, her back was burned severely, leaving opened sores that had become infected. The village people, who were helping the sick woman, used the ashes from the burned cow dung and sprinkled it in the open wound of the woman's back, thinking that would help to heal the sores. Anna asked them to take the cot out of the hut into the yard so she could examine the woman more thoroughly. The village people refused to move her, saying:

"You move her. You are a Christian. You have no caste. You can't become unclean. You move her. We can't."

Anna told her helper to take one end of the cot and they moved the women outside into the yard. Upon careful examination, the woman looked as if she had not had a bath. Her lips were dry, and her tongue was out of her mouth. Her eyelids were stiff and her bowels had not moved in over a week, which caused her abdomen to be large from constipation. When the village people saw what Anna was about to do, they were very upset. They caused such a commotion until the headman came and said:

"Keep quiet. You have not been able to help her!

So step aside and let the missionary do her work."

After first saying a prayer and asking God to guide them, they washed her face, dressed the wound on her back and proceeded to give her an enema. After all of this was done, a cloth was spread on the cot and she was laid down again. A sigh of relief was on her face as she lay on the cot in the warm sun outside the hut. Anna and Miss Whites prayed with the village people before leaving for the journey back to the mission to ask the Lord to heal this woman. Before leaving the village, Anna asked the helper to clean the hut, take the dung pots out and making sure that there was clean water to drink. The rest of the villagers looked on in amazement at the improvement that the sick lady had made in just a short visit from the missionaries.

They returned to the Mission and sent back jugs of clean water from the well for the women to drink. They told them she had to drink four to six cups of water and take the medicine they had sent back with them. A two-day supply of medicine was sent back. The liquid medicine was fruit juice from dried California fruit. The dried fruit was sent to one of our missionaries by her mother. Before the fruit arrived, the missionary's mother died, and she could not eat the fruit. Mellin's food and malted milk was the other packet of medicine sent back with them with the specific instruction of how to administer it. They dare not tell them that the medicine was food, because they would not give it to her. After about two weeks the people from the village did not come for more medicine. Anna and Miss Whities decided to visit the village to see how the lady was doing, and to their surprise, the woman was up walking around. Her back completely healed and there were not any visible scars. The whole village turned out to greet them. They wanted to worship them, saying that they had raised the women from the dead. Anna didn't want them to worship her, but instead she wanted them to praise God, for He was the one who healed her. The news quickly spread throughout the villages. It made a wonderful impression in the Karmatar district, and several schools and churches were raised up.

Anna was getting a little restless. She wanted to return to complete the work started in Simla. The procedure was to send two workers out to canvass the areas and to give the Bible studies, but since there was not another worker to go out with Anna, she persuaded Mr. Shaw to send her out alone. She was also informed that another self-supporting missionary would be arriving soon, and she would join Anna in the work in Simla.

On March 15, 1903, Anna traveled back to Simla to complete the work that she and Donna Humphrey had started. Within a few weeks the new missionary, Helen Wilcox, joined Anna in Simla. They rented the same cottage at the YWCA Holiday Home. Frieda Haegert, who worked at the YWCA, became very interested in the books and literature they were selling and began to take studies. Soon she accepted the teachings of the church and asked for Saturdays off. Her employer refused to let her have the day off and Ms. Haegert quit her job. However, this did not discourage her. She was already a salesperson, and she began working with Anna and Helen, canvassing the areas in Simla. The three pioneering ladies were very busy in all of India, traveling across the country from Calcutta to Bombay, and thirty-seven other cities, ending in Peshawar on the border of Afghanistan. Most of the time they traveled together, but on a few trips they split up so more territory could be covered. On one of those trips, Helen Wilcox went back to Calcutta. Frieda Haegert took the train that traveled the main line, and Anna took the train that traveled the back country, and other Indian states. Besides carrying all of the books and luggage, there was also a tiffin basket. A tiffin basket is a basket that food, cooking utensils and a small stove was packed in, so they could prepare their own food. They had to be very careful of the food and the water while traveling, because often times it was not safe.

On this trip Anna gave Frieda the tiffin basket to take with her. They planned to meet in two days at a railway junction. Anna felt that she could manage to find food on her own. When Anna approached the stationmaster to buy a ticket to Dhola, the agent refused to sell her the ticket. He said it was not safe for her to travel alone, and that she might get kidnapped or killed. She insisted that he sell her the ticket. After finally purchasing her ticket, Anna boarded the train, and tried to make herself comfortable for the night. All through the night someone would knock on the wall, saying, "Don't sleep; there are thieves on this train." She did not sleep on the train, but as soon as the train pulled into the station at Dhola, she went to the ladies room and made a bed on the couch and slept the remainder of the night.

The next morning, she went to look for the town, but there was none. She asked the stationmaster where the town was. He said there was none, and that they were at a railway junction. Disappointed, she asked when the next train was due. "The next morning," he said.

She wondered what she would do with all her time while waiting for the next train. She kept busy writing letters home, checking her inventory and looking over her schedule. By this time she was getting hungry, but remembered that she had given the tiffin basket to Frieda. She asked the stationmaster if he could fix her breakfast. The station servant prepared rice and curry for her, but she was not able to eat it. Not wanting to be disrespectful, she threw it out the back and paid for the meal. All she could do was say a prayer and hope that God would provide for her.

By noon she heard a train coming, thinking it was going in her direction, she hurried out to the platform to meet it. She was disappointed to learn that the train was not going to the next town where she wanted to go. Just then Anna noticed four fine-looking native men walking toward her dressed in white silk European shirts, bareheaded and barefooted. She was frightened, and the words of the stationmaster echoed in her mind, "You might get kidnapped." She stood still and prayed as they approached her.

"Salaam. Missionary?" they asked.

"Yes."

"From America?"

"Yes."

"Know Sahibs Lenker and Stroup?"

"Yes. I met them in Mount Vernon, Ohio on their return to the States while I was in school," she replied.

They carried on with the conversation and told Anna they had sold them some books, *Man, the Masterpiece.* They asked her if she had any books. Anna told them that she did and sold them *Heralds of the Morning* and *Oriental Watchman.* They were very happy to receive the books and wanted to know if she would come to their state to teach. Anna said she would pass their request on to the Mission Board. With that they re-boarded their train and went on their way.

The next morning the train arrived at the station. Anna was so glad to board the train she forgot that she had not had anything to eat or drink. The train traveled through the desert area of India. It was hot and dusty because she had the window open trying to get fresh air. They pulled into the station in order to change the crew and refuel. Anna got off the train to walk on the platform and to stretch her legs. She heard the train whistle blow and returned to the train to complete the trip. As she entered her compartment, there on the seat was a beautiful white plate with brown toast and a cup of something hot to drink. She looked around to see who placed it there, but there was no one. She prayed a prayer of thanks and proceeded to eat the food that was left on the seat. The meal satisfied her hunger and thirst. She thanked God again for taking care of her. While she was enjoying her meal, she saw a man on the platform of the train station dressed in a uniform that she had not seen before. He smiled and spoke to her in perfect English.

"I hope you enjoyed your meal".

Anna answered with a smile saying, "I certainly did."

About midafternoon, she arrived at another station where she had to change trains and wait sixteen hours to catch the British lines in order to meet Miss Haegert. As she disembarked from the train and went inside the station to freshen up, the stationmaster was surprised to see a woman traveling alone without an escort.

"What is a European woman doing here traveling alone without an escort," he asked.

"I am on the Kings business," Anna replied.

"Oh you are one of those silly missionaries trying to convert the heathens" "Do you really believe there is a God?" the stationmaster asked.

"Yes," Anna replied. "After what was done for me today, I believe more than ever there is a God."

After hearing what Anna said, he calmed down and started talking about how he came to the village to make money, and in the process lost his religion. He said that his wife was a Christian, and he wished she was with him, because she would love to talk with someone else who believed in God. But his wife was sick in a hospital in Bombay. A sad but gentle look came over his face as he told her that he may never see her again. Anna tried to assure him that if it was God's will she could get better. She told him of the miracle that God had performed for her that day and surely if He can take care of her. She sold him the books *Heralds of the Morning* and the *Oriental Watchman*. He was glad to get the books and knew that his wife would enjoy reading them. A relief came over the stationmaster and he told Anna to be careful and directed her to the waiting room.

She placed her luggage in the waiting room and paid a coolie to look after them. She took her bicycle and rode into the village to search for food and to visit the shops and bazaars, but they were closed for evening. She continued to ride around until she found the telegraph quarters. She decided to stop and go in to see if there was someone who she could canvass. To her surprise, she found two European women there. They were delighted to see her and started asking questions about why she was in the

village and if she knew a Revered Robinson. She said: yes I do".
Anna explained to them that she was a missionary and traveling
through the countryside selling books. The women said they had
purchased books from Reverend Robinson, but their subscription
had expired. Anna was glad to renew their subscriptions for them
and returned to the railway station to wait for the train to continue
her trip.

She was pleased with her visit to the small village. As she prepared to retire for the night, she heard a gentle knock at the door.
She went to see who it was and the stationmaster was standing
before her dressed in his evening clothes. She was quite surprised.
He said there was a religious meeting of natives going on in the
men's waiting room, and since she was a missionary, he thought
she might be interested. He had come to escort her there. Anna
dressed quickly and proceeded to the meeting with him.

The stationmaster and Anna were seated in two large seats at
the front of the room. The stationmaster motioned for the men to
continue with the meeting. The room was filled with people and
idols of fish, alligators, bulls and various other things, each having little altars of incense in front of them. The worshipers sat on
the floor in front of their respective idols and went through their
religious performances to weird sounds from a little hand organ
operated by a man who seemed quite different from the others.
The smoke from the incense was beginning to make her sick and
she asked to be excused. The stationmaster motioned to the leader
to stop the ceremony as Anna left for the women's waiting room.
Just before leaving, the leader of the group placed a wreath of
flowers around her neck. Anna smiled and thanked them as she
backed out of the room, afraid to turn her back on them, and went
back to the waiting room.

Early the next morning, again, there was a knock on the door.
She heard a voice saying, "Time to get up." Anna got up, packed

her things and refreshed herself to get ready for the early train. She purchased a third class ticket, although she had enough money for a first or second class ticket. She did not want the people to know she could afford a better ticket for fear of being robbed. As she boarded the train, the coolie took her luggage and bicycle to a private compartment marked "Reserved Ladies."

"This must be a mistake, I paid for a third class ticket," she told the coolie.

"No mistake" the coolie said.

When the stationmaster boarded the train to see if she was alright, Anna told him that she had paid for a third class ticket. "Enjoy yourself and be happy I ordered this compartment for you," he responded. Then she looked around and saw the stationmaster's servant coming toward the compartment with a large tray piled high with food, enough for the duration of her trip, with silverware and plates and glasses filled with lemonade and water.

When she arrived at her destination, she saw Miss Haegert waiting for her on the platform of the station, she was so glad to see her and thankful that she had a safe journey. They talked about each other's experiences while traveling on separate journeys and continued their work traveling together to Lahore. As they approached the city, Anna remembered that she had met a lady from Lahore and wrote her name and address in her book. She searched desperately for it but could not find it. All she could do was pray and ask the Lord to help them find a place to stay. Anna told Frieda to stay with their suitcases and she would take her bicycle and go into the city to see if she could search for the lady or find accommodations for them.

In Lahore, India the streets had names like cities in America. The houses also had names, and in many instances you could find the name of the persons who live in the house printed on the gate. As she rode through the streets looking for names of roads and streets, she searched for something that might jog her memory of the name of the lady. She came into the heart of the city at a place called the Mall where all the roads intersected.

"Go that way," a voice told her.

She looked around to see if anyone was near her. Seeing no one, she obeyed the voice and rode her bicycle in the direction she was told. It was as though someone or something was guiding the bicycle down the streets until finally she saw a street named, "Temple Road." "That's it," she shouted and continued to ride down the streets looking for the names on the houses. After a few blocks she saw the name "Mrs. O'Calahan." That was the name of the lady! She was happy and thankful that she found the house. The house had a large gate and she did not know how she was going to get the attention of the people who lived there. Just then the gatekeeper came up and opened the gate and let her in.

It was the custom that if you wanted to see a person who lived in the house you would place your card on the card plate and it would be presented to the individual who lived there. Anna told the servant that she did not have a card, but wanted to see the lady of the house. The servant directed her to the parlor and shortly after the lady came down dressed as if she was about to go out.

"Mrs. O'Calahan,' Anna said. "You may not remember me, but I met you before and you told me if I ever came to Lahore to be sure to look you up?" Although she remembered Anna, she said:

"I am sorry; I have only my brother's room. He just left this morning and the room is not presentable."

"Oh never mind that, let me see it," Anna said.

She showed Anna the room. This is perfect," Anna said.

Mrs. O'Calahan said: alright you may have the room".

"My friend is waiting for me at the train station. I will go and get her and let her know that I found a place to stay." Anna hurried back to the train station to tell Frieda the good news. As she approached the station Frieda could see the smile on Anna's face, she knew that she had succeeded in finding a place for them to stay.

Anna and Frieda stayed with Mrs. O'Calahan while they completed their work in Lahore. The two young Missionaries were happy to have a safe and clean place to live while they continued their work.

Anna Knight First School and Students
near Gitano, MS

Anna's Graduation
from Battle Creek Sanitarium as
Missionary Nurse

Anna and Co-worker
in Calcutta, India

Soso Adventist Church in Soso, MS
(around 1921)

Anna and Grace Home
in Jasper County, MS

Newton Knight
(Anna's Father)

Elder and Mrs. I. Dyo Chambers
who helped her to receive
her education.

Anna Knight Memorial Nurses Hostel
Giffard Memorial
Nuzvid, India (November, 2005)

Anna's Sisters
Grace and Lessie

Anna's Brother Howard and Family

Georgeanne
(Anna's Mother)

Chapter 8

❧◦◦☙

$\mathscr{A}$nna had worked in India for six and a half years traveling and seeing the exquisite beauty of the vast country. She spent each summer in Simla, going down to the plains during the winter or cool weather months. All of her travels were on the East India Railway traveling from Calcutta to Simla down across from Calcutta to Bombay, stopping in the small surrounding villages selling magazines and books to the English speaking people living there. Finding suitable and safe lodging was a constant struggle. In some instances they found themselves sleeping in the railway station's ladies waiting room. But this did not stop the two young missionaries from doing the work that they was trained to do. Anna had given up everything to work in India; her family, school and the way of life in the United States. While in India she had many experiences that she would never forget and she knew that there was someone who was protecting her as she worked to tell others about God's Love.

It was very hot in the village of Moltan, India but the heat did not stop Anna from completing her work of canvassing the sixty bungalows in the small village. The people warned her that it was too hot to be out in the sun during the day, but as usual Anna wanted to complete her task and continued to work. After a few hours of walking, she had a terrible headache. Her temperature was 105, but she continued to visit the people in the remaining bungalows. The plan was to meet Frieda in Amritsar at the railroad station the next day. When she arrived at the station, her head was hurting so bad that she could not see and passed by Frieda without speaking. Frieda asked what is wrong. Anna told her of her terrible headache and said she was going to rest for a few days. She was so sick that she thought she was going to die. She even wrote a letter to her family in Mississippi explaining to them of her illness, and that if she died, she was doing the work of the Lord. She gave the letter to Frieda stating that if she did not recover, please mail the letter to her sister Grace in Mississippi. Unable to work, she stayed in the bed for a few days while Frieda continued to work in the village. She was disappointed that Frieda had to finish visiting the bungalows in the village without her, however she had no choice but to stay in bed. After a few days of bed rest, Anna realized that she had sunstroke and it could have killed her. For about three weeks she had to wear dark glasses and stay out of the sun. It was hard for her to do, but she realized that if the work was to be completed then she must take care of herself.

On another occasion, Anna and Frieda had been traveling so much throughout India that they had not eaten fresh fruit or vegetables for weeks. Their diet consisted of dahl and rice, (which was a lentil stew) and once in while curry. They next city on the itinerary was Rawalpindi and Peshawar on the border of Afghanistan. Anna heard that there was a native bazaar that had an abundance of fresh food and other supplies that they needed. After they arrived at the place they were to stay while working in the village, the two ladies made a list of the items needed. Since Anna had the bicycle, it was her job to shop for food. Frieda was better at cooking. As she proceeded down the path to find the bazaar, she saw a large walled in place with huge gates. Upon entering the gates there were tables filled with baskets of all kinds, fresh vegetables, fruits and meats. As she was purchasing the grocery items, she noticed two tall men holding large knives following her. Anna walked in different directions within the bazaar keeping her distance to see if the men were following her. Thinking that this could be trouble, she quickly completed her shopping and returned to her bicycle and placed all the fruits and vegetables in the basket. She rode down the path as fast as she could, making sure to ride on the main street. If the men continued to follow her, other people could see if she called for help. Arriving home safely, the landlady was shocked and surprised. She told her that Europeans were not allowed in that market and it was a wonder that she was not killed and warned her never to do that again. Anna knew that there was someone who was watching out for her.

There were many customs in the Hindu culture and if you were not familiar with them the Hindu people could be easily offended. One day, Anna wanted to start her Bible studies early and went down to the servant's quarters to request the rickshaw. When she arrived at their hut, the servants were sitting down ready to eat breakfast. Immediately they jumped to their feet and pushed their breakfast aside. The servants took Anna to her destination and waited for her. When Anna completed the Bible Studies, she noticed that the servants were in the bazaar talking loudly among themselves. She asked "What is all the commotion about?" They replied: "You had us to work all day without any food."

The leader told her that when she came to their hut, they were ready to eat their morning meal. When she opened the door the sun was at her back and cast a shadow upon them and their food. That shadow had spoiled the food, and made them unclean. According to their customs a Hindu cannot eat food on which a Christian's shadow has fallen. Anna apologized for offending them and asked what she could do to correct the situation. After giving them a generous tip, about fifty cents, they were able to pay the priest in the temple to make them clean again. Anna never disturbed the servants again at their mealtime.

Elder J. Shaw and his wife were working in Calcutta, Elder Shaw became very sick. He could not receive the medical care needed in India. They decided to return to the United States and Anna was asked to return to Calcutta to help the Shaw's pack. She assisted them in packing and saw to it that they boarded the ship leaving for America. Anna was very sad to see them leave but knew that this was best for both of them.

It was late at night and Anna took the train back to Moltan, India which was about one hundred and sixty-seven miles. She made herself comfortable in her compartment and laid down to sleep, placing her collar, bow tie, Bible and a watch that Mr. Chambers had given her in her handbag. She placed the handbag under her seat thinking it would be safe. During the night, someone entered the compartment and stole her handbag. When she realized what had happened she was heartbroken, especially about the Bible and watch, because they were items that were given to her by Mr. Chambers. They were very precious to her. Learning from that experience, she never again placed her handbag under her seat, instead she placed it under her pillow.

Another experience that was very troubling for Anna was when she was traveling by train through the town of Dinapure. A well-dressed man in a white silk shirt and dhoti (native shirt) came to her compartment for ladies only. In India, the ladies and men were always separated in public. With him were a lady and two small beautiful girls about seven or eight year's old dressed in white saris with faces veiled. When the lady and the two small girls were safely inside the compartment, the man stood in the doorway.

"You will see that no men come into this compartment, will you not?" he said.

"Sure!" Anna replied, not knowing exactly what she was

agreeing to. The man felt assured and closed the door and proceeded down to another compartment marked men only.

As the train started to move, the young ladies removed their veils. Anna noticed that each of the girls had a red mark from the center of the forehead down between the eyes to the nose. There was an Anglo-Indian lady in the compartment, Anna said:

"How strange they both were hurt alike!"

"No," the lady said. "They are not hurt. That is paint on their faces."

"Why would they do that to these beautiful children?" Anna asked.

"Just as we wear a wedding ring, they put that red paint on when they get married."

"Do you mean to tell me these girls are married?"

"Yes," the lady replied.

The young girls realized they were talking about them.

"Your hands have no ring," one of the girls said.

"I am not married," Anna replied.

"Not married? How old are you?"

"About to turn forty." The lady and the girls looked very surprised.

"Too late, too late. You should be a grandmother by now."

These two little girls were engaged and married by their parents to boys ten and twelve years old. The little girls were on their way to their mother-in-law's house to be trained as wives. They will stay with their in-laws never to see their husbands until their wedding day. Oh how happy she was that she lived in a country that did not have this kind of culture. Anna never married. She dedicated her life to God and continued to do His work.

Anna was busy with the literature work in India, but, she never forgot about her family and the people at home. She stayed in contact with her family in Mississippi as much as possible. She received a letter in the mail from her sister Grace, saying that the school was burned down. Tears came to her eyes and she wondered why she was in India, when her own people were suffering back home because a lack of education. Anna was so hurt and worried about her school that she wrote the General Conference in the United States telling them of the situation at home, and asked for a furlough to return to Mississippi. Anna traveled back to Calcutta to await a response to her request. She reflected on the work that was done in India. She kept a journal, and in it she recorded all the trips made, miles traveled, expenses, books and literature that were sold. She worked very hard every day trying to make each day better than the one before for the people she came in contact with. She was thankful for the experiences that she had working with the people in the small towns and villages, as well as the large cities. As she looked back on the work, her only regret was that she had not been able to do more.

Mission Field of Mississippi

Chapter 9

Anna continued her work in India, knowing that the school and the people back home in Mississippi were suffering. They did not have anyone to teach them and the schoolhouse was burned down. She had tried all that she could to get someone to carry on the work of teaching the children. Several people tried, but were met with opposition from the moonshiners and the Knight Riders. Letters had been written to friends and conference officials, but there was not a person who could continue on with the school.

Upon returning from a long day of giving studies to the people in a small village, she noticed a letter on the table addressed to her. The letter was postmarked from Mississippi. It looked as if it was written by a child. With trembling hands she opened the letter.

Dear Anna,

Why don't you come back and teach us yourself? You understand us and you are not afraid. Why are you staying over there trying to convert the heathens in India, while your own people here at home are growing up to be heathens?

The letter haunted her for several weeks. She tried to forget about it but the words kept coming back in her mind. Anna wrote the Conference Officials again and told them if they could not find someone to take over her school in Mississippi, then please grant her request for a furlough.

Anna was filled with mixed emotions. Even though she had requested the leave, she kept thinking about all the boys and girls she had taught at the Mission School in Karmatar, and the people who had given their hearts to Christ as a result of her literature evangelist work. She also thought about her good friend and co-worker Donna Humphrey who died while working in India. But in her heart she knew that she had to answer the call for help from her own people. After several months a letter was received from the Office of Missions of the General Conference granting her request for a furlough.

As she prepared to leave India, she left her bicycle and other belongings at the Karmatar Mission School for safe keeping until her return. The Mission workers gave her a going away party and money for her trip home. They were very sad to see her go but they understood the reason she was leaving and accepted her promise that she would return to finish the work.

As she boarded the ship in Calcutta in August, 1907 to start the journey back to America and her home in Mississippi, she looked at the people who were standing on the dock waving good-bye to her. She thought about all the wonderful memories of her work in India.

Anna did not travel on a luxury liner, but by cargo ships. The fare was cheaper, it was enjoyable and there were many stops at different ports along the way. The cargo ships did not go straight to America, and sometimes she had to wait to catch the next cargo ship that was going to her destination. This allowed her time for sightseeing in Europe. When she arrived in London, she was informed that there was two week wait for the next ship bound for America. Anna was not overly concerned about the delay. It was a good time to visit Museums, Buckingham Palace and the House of Parliament. She really took time to enjoy all the many historical places that she had studied about and saw pictures of, now she was actually visiting the sites. What a wonderful experience she could tell her students about. She bought several postcards and took pictures of the places she visited to show to her relatives and students.

Before she left India, she wrote home to tell everyone that she was headed home on furlough to build a new school house in the middle of the Community. One of her uncles, John Early Knight, provided one acre of land for the new school building. Every able bodied person in Six Town worked on the new school building trying to complete it before Anna arrived home.

The voyage back to America gave her plenty of time to think and plan for the new school that was being built. She was very excited because it was going to be a new day for the "Knight Family" and others in the community. When she finally reached New York in November, 1907, she wrote home again telling her relatives to rush the work of building the school because she would be home in two weeks and wanted to start school right away.

On her way to Mississippi Anna stopped by the General Conference Headquarters in Washington DC. The officials were very glad to see her and were eager to hear about her work in India. While in Washington DC, she spent a few days at the Washington Sanitarium for a checkup and also visited old friends in the area. She continued on her trip home, but stopped in Chattanooga, Tennessee expecting to see Mrs. L. Dyo Chambers, the lady who helped her to finish school to become a Missionary Nurse. When she arrived at the home of Mrs. Chambers, a lady answered the door. Anna told her who she was and asked to see Mrs. Chambers. The lady informed Anna that Mrs. Chambers died two weeks earlier. Anna was heartbroken. She wanted so much to tell her all about her experiences in India and to thank her for helping and believing in her. She went to the cemetery to visit her grave and whispered a prayer of thanks.

While in the area she visited Mr. and Mrs. Atwood. They were the couple who tried to teach at her school in Gitano when Anna went to India. She spent two days visiting with the Atwood's to catch up with all the news that happened while she was in India. They were just as excited to hear about her work in the foreign mission field. The Atwood's apologized to Anna because they could not continue to teach at the school, but they just could not live in fear for their lives all the time. While in the Chattanooga area, Anna shopped for supplies for the school. She knew that she could not find some of the items she needed in Mississippi and decided to purchase a few items to take with her. Later in the afternoon on a Thursday, the Atwood's took her to the station to catch the train for Ellisville, Mississippi.

On Friday afternoon she arrived in Ellisville. Her brother Howard and other relatives were there to meet her with a span of mules and a spring wagon. They were so glad to see her that they gave her a big hug and handed her a sack lunch that Anna's mother had prepared for her. The trip to her home in Six Town was much quicker and more comfortable. She enjoyed the ride home and talked with her brother about what was going on with the rest of the family and the people in her hometown. The next day, her mother prepared a wonderful meal of Anna's favorite foods, welcoming her back home. Family members came by throughout the day to say hello and to say how glad they were to see her.

The first Sunday after her arrival, the whole community was at the new school house to welcome her back. Even the people responsible for burning the old school were there; some were sitting down with the rest of people and the others were standing outside looking in. Anna was telling the students about her experiences in India and all the places she had visited. She showed the pictures and the postcards to them. The students were so excited to have her back home to teach them. They never thought the little "green girl" from Mississippi could ever go to all those faraway places and do all the things she talked about. In concluding her remarks Anna said, "Now I've told you all of this in order that you may understand better what it means for me to leave India and come back home to try to help you. This country has everything compared to India. You are living in virtual luxury compared to the people in India, and yet I know you need help too. No one knows that better than I do. I have come back because you are my blood brothers and sisters, uncles, aunts, cousins, nieces and nephews; we are all kinfolk. I hope you understand what we are here for today. Remember, you have come a long way from where you were in 1898, when none of you could read or write. Now, with what I did for you before I left for India and what Brother and Sister Atwood did for you until they had to go, your outlook on life is brighter. If you will co-operate with the Lord through me, there will be still brighter and better days ahead. You, however, must be willing to work hard. Parents you must buy books for each school child; each grade will require different books and tuition has to be paid. Then, there will be papers in addition to the books. Each family must subscribe to *Our Little Friend,* or the *Youth's Instructor*, as the need arises. Another thing, there will not be time for any side lines. What I mean by that is, no card parties, no dances and other questionable forms of amusement. If you are all willing to comply with this program and attend school regularly, I am willing and ready to do all I can to help you. If not, then say so now. Let me see those who will co-operate with me in this work please stand." Everyone stood. Anna was surprised because she knew how they enjoyed dancing and having parties. Okay, she said, school will start bright and early Monday morning at eight o'clock. Please bring all your books or pieces of books paper and pencils or whatever you have, we will work with the items until supplies can be ordered.

That Monday morning, the sun was shining, the birds were singing as if to say "thank you Anna". Twenty-two students arrived ready to learn with tuition in hand. Anna did not know what grades the students were in, but she tested each one and placed each student in the right grade. The school was not completely finished but classes could be held in the building

The area in Jasper County where the school was located is known as the Pine Belt Region because of the abundance of tall pine trees. Conditions had changed in the community of Six Town. The people were able to sell their timber to the companies from the North and were paid a handsome price. This enabled the parents to pay for the books and tuition for their children. After school was dismissed, the workmen came to complete the work with help from the neighbors and family members.

The school was going very well. Books and other supplies were ordered. The school hours were long with one hour for lunch and no recess except for the little ones who could have a break in the afternoon. The students did not seem to mind, they had waited so long for someone to teach them and were willing to do anything to learn. The school building was finally finished. Anna and the students planted flowers in the front yard to make the entrance welcoming. The school was for grades one thru six. By the sixth grade, the students felt that they had all the learning needed.

Anna resumed her Sunday school and Young People's Society program in the Soso community about six miles away. After about six months, nine people were ready for baptism; her mother Georgeann, two sisters Lessie and Grace, a niece and their cousin, plus four others, including a Methodist Minister, were among the group of believers and were observing Saturday as the Sabbath. There were still about twenty-six people attending the meetings every Sunday. Truly the light was beginning to shine in Jones County, Mississippi.

In the early spring and summer, there was no school because the families needed everybody to help plant the crops. The students were told to continue to study the books they had in order to be ready in the fall when school started again. In the meantime, Anna was asked by the Southeastern Conference President to visit the other companies and small churches in the area to encourage them and to conduct Bible studies. The churches were always happy when Anna visited. She told them about her work in India. To see a person who actually had gone out of the United States was amazing to the people. They listened intently to her many experiences about working in India. They were very interested in the school that was started in the Gitano area. There was another community near Sumrall where her aunt Augusta Watts lived that was very interested in receiving Bible studies. Anna wrote her aunt a letter telling her that she was coming for a visit and to have the interested people to meet at her home. She traveled there by bus. Her cousins picked her up from the bus station in the horse and buggy and took her to their modest home about eight miles outside of Sumrall. She had planned to spend only one night, but she stayed for three days. They were so interested in the studies they invited their neighbors to come to study with them. This resulted in the planting of another church in the area. There was no Pastor assigned to the church to lead them, but they were not discouraged and they continued on with Lay Minister until a Minister was assigned to their group.

The Colored work in American was just beginning to blossom. There was a growing need for someone to reach the people in the south to tell them about the love of God. Anna was still trying to decide if she should return to India where the need was also great, or stay in America and work with the people where she lived.

Her two-year furlough was just about up and she was completing another school year. Anna was training her sister Grace who was seventeen years old to take over the school. The students were grasping all the knowledge they were being taught, and most never missed a day. She felt that she had accomplished a lot in the two years. The moonshiners and other people in the community who doubted her teachings and techniques were beginning to settle down. There was no more trouble.

Southeastern Union Conference

The Colored Department

Chapter 10

A letter arrived for Anna from the secretary of the Southeastern Union Conference in Atlanta, Georgia. It was an offer for a position as a Medical Matron of a new Sanitarium being built for the colored people in the city of Atlanta. Although Anna was capable of operating the Sanitarium, she wanted to know who suggested her name. She first thought it was a plan from some of the people who wanted her to stay in the United States and finish the work among her people in the South. On the other hand it could have been someone who knew the commitment to her work in India and the work she was doing in Mississippi.

There was only one thing to do; she had to find out who suggested her name. She took the letter and in the privacy of her room she asked God for a sign. If it was the people who wanted her to stay in the United States and not go back to India, then she knew it was man's plan. If it was from the two individuals, Elder G. A. Irwin or Elder C.P. Bollman, both from the General Conference and who knew her well and the work that she was doing, then she would know that it was God's will that she accept the position.

After praying earnestly, she wrote a letter to R. T. Dowsett, the secretary of the Southeastern Union Conference asking him for the name or names of the person who had recommended her. She waited patiently for an answer before she would commit to the position as Medical Matron. Within a few days she had her answer; it was Elder G. A. Irwin and a few others who recommended her. Anna was pleased that it was Elder Irwin and she knew that it was God's plan for her to take the position.

First, she wrote the General Conference office to tell them about her new job offer from the Southeastern Conference and that she wanted to accept. Everyone agreed that it would be easier to find someone to go to India to continue the work there than to find someone who could help establish the colored work in Atlanta. The General Conference gladly gave Anna permission to stay in the United States.

Anna wrote back to Elder Dowsett and told him that she would accept the offer to be the Medical Matron at the Sanitarium that was starting in the city. She also told him that it would take her a few days to organize the work in Mississippi and she would be on her way. Her family and relatives were sorry to see her leave, but they knew that this was a great opportunity for her and they were proud of the "Little Green Girl from Mississippi" who was called to do this important job. Anna felt confident leaving the School in the hands of her sister Grace. She had trained her sister very well and felt that the school would go on in the community. There was also a small company of Sabbath keepers in Sumrall and they were continuing to grow. Anna was pleased with the work she was doing with the small companies of Sabbath Keepers in the surrounding area.

Within a few days she received a check to cover the cost of her transportation and other expenses. She packed a few belongings and left for Atlanta, Georgia. On the train ride to Atlanta she was wondering what she would find when she reached her destination. She had no instructions of what to do other than to be the Medical Matron. She did not know the condition of the new Sanitarium, nor did she know the living arrangements. All she knew was to go to Atlanta, Georgia.

When she arrived in Atlanta a car was sent to pick her up and take her to the house at 209 Greensferry Avenue. She found it empty, unfurnished, unfinished, cold and dreary. "What had she gotten herself into", she thought. Was this supposed to be the new Sanitarium? She had to pray to ask God for guidance on how she was to do this work with very little to work with. She did not know anyone in the city who she could call to provide her with information on how to proceed with the work she was called to do. She knew that there were two teachers at the mission school which was organized by Elder G. E. Peters in the Second Seventh-day Adventist Church. She contacted one of the teachers to ask where she should go to start the work. The lady did not have an answer for her. Anna prayed some more and was beginning to wonder if she was really needed in Atlanta. The teachers invited her to stay with them for a few days until she could find out what her mission was in the big city of Atlanta. Anna called the Southeastern Conference Office to inform them that she was in the city and was ready to go to work. She asked if there were any funds available to help furnish and clean the house on Greensferry. The answer was no, she had to do whatever she could with the money that was left from her expense money. Anna looked over the house and made a list of the items she needed right away to get started. She went to a local store and purchased a two burner gasoline stove, then went to the second hand store and bought a bed, a new Red Cross mattress and a few other items, then began housekeeping. She cleaned and scrubbed the walls and floors until they were presentable. She painted the bed frame white to make it look like new. Within a few weeks the mission house on Greensferry Avenue was inviting. The treatment rooms were nicely furnished with all the necessary equipment for regular treatments such as hot and cold water, shower, spray, and electric-light bath, nice towels and sheets, all ready to receive patients.

What Anna did not know was that a group of people in the community opposed the opening and the operation of a Sanitarium and had circulated a petition. The area was surrounded by several black colleges such as Morehouse, Spelman, Morris Brown, Clark and Atlanta University. Atlanta was a city with quite of few of black elite and this was their neighborhood. You could tell the students from the surrounding colleges were different from all other blacks living in Atlanta. The Morehouse men always dressed in suits and ties and the Spelman ladies were dressed with fancy dresses and gloves whenever they shopped or attended other events. The neighborhood consisted of College Professors, Doctors, Business Owners and they did not want a Sanitarium in their community. They took their petition to the Mayor and received an injunction against the operation of the Sanitarium. Choosing not to offend the residents of the neighborhood by operating the Greensferry Avenue Sanitarium, she went to the Conference Officials to see if they could approve her to operate a private treatment room in her home as a nurse. This was agreeable to them. In addition to operating a treatment room in her home, the conference officials felt that she should take on the responsibility of a Bible instructor for the colored people in Atlanta. Sister Osborne, who was white, was presently the Bible Worker in the colored community. She had made contact with a few people who were interested in learning more. Sister Osborne gave her all of her materials to Anna for her to follow up with the individuals and she went to another part of the Atlanta to work.

The treatment room was not doing well; people had never heard of water and electrical treatments and did not want to try it. Anna heard of a lady who was very ill and the Doctors had done all they could to cure her of a severe cold. Anna contacted her and asked if her Doctor did not object, she would like to try her treatments. The Doctor came to visit Anna to discuss with her the lady's condition. He had done all he could and to go ahead with the treatment. The lady was so sick and she was willing to try anything to get well, so she began the treatments. Anna started with fomentation cloths and deep breathing. In a few days the lady was sitting up and in a week she was well. The lady told other people in the community about her treatment at the Sanitarium and how she was healed as a result of the treatment received from Nurse Anna.

The G. E. Peters Mission School in the city of Atlanta was doing very well. The night classes were running out of room. Anna was chairman of the school board and she had to come up with a way to accommodate all the students who wanted to attend the school. The school did not have the necessary funds to continue to operate. Anna went to the Conference Office again, to see if they had any funds available to help out with purchasing desks and other materials to meet the needs of the growing school. They said they had none because they were already paying half of the teacher's salary. Then she asked if they would permit her to buy the items needed on credit, and they approved. She was saving money for a winter coat, but thought that God would keep her warm. Anna used the funds that she was saving for her coat to buy the items needed for the school. She went to the hardware store, selected a stove, made the down payment and promised to pay toward the balance until it was paid in full. Next were the desks. She had put a good amount of money as down payment for the stove and had little left for the desks. Going out on faith she went to the school supply house and told them what was needed and the amount of money she had for the down payment. After a brief discussion, the supplier agreed to sell her the desks with the understanding that the balance would be paid in installments until paid. The stove and desks were delivered to the school as promised. Everyone was so happy but they knew that they were in debt. Anna assured them that the Lord had blessed them so far and He would not fail them now. She prayed that the parents would pay their tuition fees so that their obligations could be met. Without fail the parents paid the tuition and they were able to pay back the suppliers as promised. Again, the Lord will never fail when doing His Will.

Anna did not have money for her coat and it was colder in Atlanta than in Mississippi, there was nothing else to do but to start saving again for a coat. A few weeks later she was answering letters from friends and she came across one from Mrs. Edith Embree- Runnels, the person who sent her the *Signs of the Times*, she was a good friend and they had corresponded over the years. In her letter, Anna told her about all the experiences she was having in Atlanta, including the private treatment room, the school that was started and how she had to spend the money that she was saving for a winter coat to buy school supplies. She told her that the work must come first. A few weeks later Anna received a letter from Edith, and she told her that she read her letter to the Missionary Volunteer Society in her home church, and they wanted to send her a donation to help with the work. Also, to Anna's surprise she received an express package containing a beautiful black broad-cloth coat. She was very happy and was reminded, "But my God shall supply all your needs according to his riches in glory by Christ Jesus."

Word was getting around the colored community of Atlanta about Anna's work. She was making quite a few friends with the elite establishment. Anna began to visit the colored colleges in the Atlanta area and was asked by the wife of the President of Atlanta Baptist College to visit the colored summer schools of Atlanta to lecture to the young girls on "Social Purity" and also speak at the

State Baptist Sunday School Convention. The Baptist Committee thought that Anna was the right person to do this. In order for her to do all the work that she was called to do, it was important for her to earn the trust and the respect of the colored people. It was hard work but that was nothing new to Anna. After all, she had been a hard worker all of her life.

On May 13, 1912 the G. E. Peters School had a beautiful and well attended closing program in the church. The church was decorated with beautiful and colorful flowers and filled to capacity. With the tuition and donations received that year they were able to pay off the debts and had a cash balance of $2.24. As she looked back over the six years that the school was established, that was the best year. Her heart overflowed with gratitude for all the prayers from friends who aided in the work.

Chapter 11

$\mathscr{T}$he G. E. Peters School in Atlanta had just completed a successful year with enrollment of ninety-five students. Anna had made many influential friends in Atlanta; continued to be invited to speak at the local colleges and other meetings. In conversations with a group of ladies, she asked why there was not a colored branch of the Young Women's Christian Association (YWCA). There was a colored branch of the YMCA for the men. Having been a member of the YWCA in India and knowing the good work it did, she thought a branch for women would go very well in Atlanta. Since she could not operate a sanitarium in the building on Greensferry Street the way that was planned, she thought that the building could be used for a YWCA. It was already being used to conduct Bible Classes, a night school, a reading room, and providing temporary rooms for working young ladies to stay. In essence it was already a YWCA so why not make it an official organization? Again, Anna took her vision to God in prayer and asked for His guidance to establish a place for women of Atlanta to learn and to prepare them for entering into society.

A meeting was called with the women who were staying at the Greensferry house and the people who were attending the night school. The idea of organizing a colored branch of the Young Women's Christian Association was presented to them. They were very excited and enthusiastic. She explained to the group that this plan had to be presented to her Conference Officials first, because she was employed by them. She worked out a plan as to how she was going to present it to the Conference Officials to get their approval. A meeting was requested with the head of the departments. Since Anna was responsible for the colored work, she thought this would be a good way of removing some of the prejudices that had built up against Seventh-day Adventist.

The plan was presented and the conference officials granted her request, providing that it would not interfere with the other duties that had been assigned to her. Also, they specifically stated that the organization needed to operate without any obligation or cost to the Conference. Anna agreed to abide by their decision and called a meeting of the group to give them the good news that they could go ahead with organizing the first colored branch of the Young Women's Christian Association in Atlanta.

She wrote the national headquarters in New York City requesting literature and the guidelines for operating a YWCA branch. Immediately they had one of the local colleges, Morris Brown, to print leaflets that were to be distributed to people in the city. Special invitations were sent out to women she had met in the city, asking them to meet at a mutual place for the purpose of organizing the YWCA. At the first organizational meeting, seventeen officers were elected as the Board of Directors from all religious denominations. It was known as the "Colored Young Women's Christian Association", City Division located at 209 Greensferry Avenue, Atlanta, GA. This was in 1913. The organization grew rapidly during the first year. There were seventy-five to one hundred members from all social class.

The meetings were held once a month on Sunday afternoon at different churches in the city. Notices were sent out to the members inviting them to attend the meetings and to remind them of their dues which was paid in money or stamps. Included in the meeting notice letter was a tract about God or Health Temperance. There was always a special topic to be discussed at each meeting, such as Health and Temperance, Social Purity and Personal Hygiene. This topic was of special interest to the group; Anna was very experienced with each one because she had studied topics at Battle Creek Sanitarium. The pastor of the church where the meeting was held was invited to speak at the meetings. There was always an open question and answer period at the close of each meeting.

Several programs and classes were being taught at the YWCA for young ladies who could not attend and receive training in the local colleges because of financial reasons. The city was also so segregated they could not attend the classes being taught across town at the white branch of the YWCA. The classes were welcome assets to the black community and more women were attending. Additional teachers had to be added to help teach the classes. On some evenings there was standing room only but that did not discourage the women, they were learning so much for the nominal fee that was being charged. The most attended class was the First Aid and Home Nursing course that was taught by Anna. As a graduate of the Battle Creek Sanitarium she was well qualified to teach this course. As a result of the training classes, two women who attended the night school, one from the largest Methodist church in the city and a deaconess from the largest Baptist church who completed the course, passed the first year's nurses' examination at Morris Brown College and graduated. If it had not been for the classes that they attended at the YWCA, they may not have been able to have that wonderful opportunity. They credited the night classes which they attended for their success and encouraged others to seek out the classes being taught at the YWCA.

Anna was still carrying on the work for the Conference, overseeing the mission school as well as teaching classes at night at the YWCA. The YWCA was going so well that Anna thought it would be beneficial for them to affiliate with the national YWCA, headquartered in New York City. She wrote a letter inquiring as to how to proceed to do this. They invited her to attend a convention that was being held in Baltimore, Maryland so she could present her request to the committee. Anna traveled to Baltimore to attend the convention of the YWCA, and was very impressed with the number of people representing different Young Women's Christian Associations at the convention. Anna had her presentation ready and with anything else she had done throughout her life, she took it to God in prayer. In her presentation she explained to them that she was the organizer and a Seventh-day Adventist, the organization consisted of members from nearly all the black churches in the Atlanta area. The Association was operated in accordance with the guideline provided them by the National Headquarters of the YWCA. They commended her for her work but felt that since the Seventh-day Adventist Church was not a member of the Federation of Churches and it seemed that the Association was being largely operated by her church, they could not affiliate with the national Association of YWCA, even though the YWCA was considered non-denominational. Anna was disappointed; she presented the news to the Association and offered to resign. The group was not having it, she was the one who had the vision of starting the Young Women's Christian Association, so many young ladies were being helped; there would be no more talk of her resigning.

The Colored Young Women' Christian Association of Atlanta continued to operate the programs for young women of the community without being affiliated with the national association. It provided much needed classes to help young ladies to obtain meaningful jobs in new fields which ordinarily they could not get into because of lack of funds and education. They were contributing as much money as they could to keep the programs going and more and more people were attending the classes. Boarding rooms at the house on Greensferry Avenue were always full, providing temporary housing until individuals could save enough money to obtain their own place. It was beginning to take on a life of itself. Word was getting around in Atlanta about the good work that the colored branch was doing, the white branch of the YWCA was beginning to take notice. The Colored Young's Women's Christian Association organized and under the leadership of Anna Knight laid the foundation for the Phyllis Wheatley YWCA of Atlanta Georgia.

Anna was busy with her Bible Studies as well as teaching classes at night, all the while working with the school in Atlanta. The Greensferry house was located in walking distance to black colleges—Spelman College, school for young girls, Morehouse College school for young men, Morris Brown and Atlanta University. Atlanta was very segregated at the time but there was a thriving black business community. Very prominent doctors, lawyers and other professional businesses that catered to the black population in the city lived and worked in this area of Southwest Atlanta. On the campuses of the colleges there were always programs such as lyceums, special concerts, and lectures that were a pleasure to attend. She had many friends among the faculty members and wives of the largest churches in the city; she was invited to attend these events. Sometimes she felt out of place because they were very well dressed and she could not afford the fine clothes, but she put on her finest and enjoyed every event. Her experiences as the first black missionary to India, was of special interest to the college community. Not only was she asked to speak about her work in India, but also on health and grace for women. Anna felt that the work of the Young Women' Christian Association could now be carried on by the board and its members. She could devote more time to her work within the colored department of the Union Conference.

Under her leadership of the Colored Department of the Union Conference she added many new members to the church, tithe and offerings doubled and the school was doing well. Elder G. E. Peters who was the principle had about ninety to one hundred students enrolled in the school. It was her prayer that the people of Atlanta realized how fortunate they were to be able to get an education and to pay it forward by helping someone else.

Chapter 12

After a few years of diligently working in the city of Atlanta, Anna decided to take a break and go home to visit her sister Grace in Mississippi. She also wanted to see how the school was going and to offer any help if needed. Her brother Howard as usual met her at the train station in Ellisville, which was about twenty-six miles from her hometown of Six Town. It was a long and bumpy ride home, but she enjoyed every minute of it looking out at the tall pine trees, and passing farm land that was being harvested. She was remembering the hot days that she had spent working the fields, but now she had a difference kind of field to work. The school known as the Gitano School was not under the Southern Missionary Society of the Church, but was considered a private school operating under the standards of the Adventist Church. She gave the school children and some adults physical examinations. This was welcomed by all, since there was not a doctor or nurse in the community. She enjoyed the time that was spent with her mother Georgeann, her younger sisters Grace and Lessie, her brother Howard and his family, and other relatives. Her mother was especially glad to see her and made sure that she cooked all the food that Anna enjoyed. On this visit her mother, Georgeann called all her children together and decided to prepare her will. The will was prepared on December 20, 1920 stating:

I Georgann Knight, who being in sound mind this 20th day of December, 1920 do will and bequeath to my three daughters, Anna, Grace and Lessie as follows:

I will and bequeath to Grace the forty acres of land on which the house stands, also all of its contents, such as beds, quilts, and other furniture all the kitchen utensils and everything pertaining to household goods.

I will bequeath my two daughters, Anna and Lessie forty acres of land each of the eighty acres that remain to be decided and agreed upon by them as to who shall have the north forty acres and who shall have the south forty acres.;

Further, I will and bequeath my son Howard who already received his land inheritance of the estate when he reached the majority age twenty-one years of age and married, and he shall not come into or inherit with my daughters any part of what remains of my land, but I will bequeath to him my gun, my first looking glasses, old Log cabin quilt and a skirt that I had when he was a baby.

I appoint Anna Knight, my eldest daughter, executor of this, my last will and testament.

I Georgeann Knight do hereby declare and publish this to be my last will and only will and testament and do herby affix my seal. This 20th Day of December, 1920.

Anna and her siblings did not have any concerns with the will that their mother had prepared. In fact they were glad it was done when everyone was together. Anna stayed a few days longer than she had planned. She visited with her father Newton Knight and he wanted to hear about the work she was doing in Atlanta. She never forgot the advice he gave her when she left home to go to Chattanooga: "When someone asks who you are, just say nothing." This was exactly what she did. Family members came by to see Anna, they loved to hear her talk about the work she was doing in the big city of Atlanta, especially the important people she was meeting.

After a week visiting with her family, she returned to Atlanta and resumed her work. Her mother prepared a care package for her, canned fruits and vegetables and packed a lunch to eat on the train ride back to Atlanta. She also gave her one of her quilts to make sure that she stayed warm, since Atlanta was colder than Mississippi. As Anna boarded the train to return, she gave extra-long hugs to her family, especially to her mother, because she did not know when she would see them again. Her mother was getting frail and Anna was worried about her. She told her sister Grace to keep her informed on her health. Upon her return to Atlanta, she again resumed her work with the Mission School, Home & Health Classes at the YWCA, and Bible Studies.

It was quickly realized that a greater emphasis had to be placed on the colored race in the south, to teach them to know about the love of God. A meeting was called by the Southeastern Union Conference president Elder O. Montgomery to discuss how and who was to do this important work. During the meeting it was agreed that a black evangelist should be hired to conduct evangelist meetings in the larger cities among the southern states. A person was needed to conduct the missionary work such as visit the churches, schools, hold institutes, organize groups for missionary work and teach home-nursing classes. The committee felt that a woman should hold this position, the question was, who? Elder C. G. Manns stood up and said, "We have someone in our midst now who is capable of handling this job, she is none other than our secretary, Sister Anna Knight." The members of the Southeastern Union Conference Committee unanimously agreed. Anna was voted in as the Missionary Society Secretary. History was made that day among the Adventist Work, the first woman to serve as the Missionary Society Secretary. Elder G. E. Peters was to serve as the evangelist for the Colored Department of the church.

In 1913 she was elected as associate Home Missionary Secretary for the Southeastern Union Conference. Reviewing all the responsibilities that this new position entailed, Anna felt that she needed more training in organizing the churches into departments in order to function as smooth as possible. She requested a meeting with Elder O. Montgomery and laid out her plans. Realizing that this was new territory, Elder Montgomery sent for Mrs. Edith Graham, the Home Missionary Secretary for the world headquarters, to come to Atlanta and present a training institute for the newly created positon of the Southeast Union Conference. The institute carefully outlined the work of organizing a church and each one attending received a manual to follow.

Anna was accustomed to starting with very little means to accomplish the work at hand. She was determined to succeed and immediately planned how she was going to organize the work with the help of God to do just that. She started the Home Missionary Work at the Atlanta Church, because she knew the members. Within a few months they were trained and ready to go to work. With her own money she purchased the materials that were needed for organizing the departments of the church, and in some cases sold them at cost to the church department. There was no office except for her trunk and suitcase. The young people volunteered to help occasionally. Working under those circumstances she kept good records by hand, writing letters, financial reports to the Union Conference, and doing what had to be done.

Every year the Conference had a camp meeting, which was a gathering of all the members of the church, to come together in one place to be revived and reenergized. The Southeastern camp meeting was held in Florida which lasted about a week or longer. On the camp ground, large tents were erected for the meetings, a tent for the children and the youth, and a separate tent for the cafeteria.

As Anna was making her plans to attend, she fell down a stairway and injured her ankle. She reset her ankle and gave all the treatments that were needed. She was not going to let anything stop her from attending the camp meeting. She boarded the train headed for St. Petersburg Florida and thought, since she would be sitting on the train, it would help her ankle. When she arrived at her destination, she was mistaken, when she looked at her ankle, she could see that it was badly swollen and very painful. She was determined that her injury was not going to stop her from attending all the meetings. She gave her lectures and reports at the Missionary Volunteer, and Home Missionary departments, attended the meeting enduring great pain. Using her umbrella as a walking cane she completed her responsibilities. She especially enjoyed going to the children's tents to tell them stories about her work in India. They listened intently and for a few moments she did not feel any pain. Two ladies who were attending the camp meeting, Mrs. Mobley and Mrs. Walker noticed that her ankle was still badly swollen and tried to persuade her to get medical help and to stay off her feet. She explained to them that as long as she could travel she had to keep working; for the work was great and the laborers were few. The ladies said they would pray that the Lord would heal her ankle. Anna thanked them for their concern and prayers and proceeded to board the train for her next destination.

The next stop on her schedule was Charleston, South Carolina. Her ankle was still swollen and painful. Nevertheless she prayed and continued on her journey. She stayed at the home of one of the members of the church in Charleston. It was very comfortable and she tried to get a little rest, but her mind was on the work that had to be done in the short time she was to spend there. The next morning she realized that the church was a mile from where she was staying, and there was not a streetcar in the area. The lady at the home offered to call a taxi for her, but she refused it, because the money saved could be used toward missions. She started to walk to the church on the Sabbath morning, enduring much pain, when all of a sudden she felt lightheaded then turned around quickly on the sprained ankle. To her surprise there was no pain. She thought, "What just happened?" She put all her weight on the ankle and still there was no pain. She had just witness and felt a miraculous healing that morning. She thanked God and continued on her journey to the church. A few days later she received a letter from Mrs. Mobley inquiring about her ankle. She immediately answered her letter telling her about the experience she had. Mrs. Mobley and Mrs. Walker stated at that very hour, they prayed for a healing. Oh what a joy it is to pray for one another.

Her responsibility for the colored work in the Southeastern Union Conference required her to travel to different churches and schools throughout the regions. She knew that education was the key for colored folk to survive during this era. She made it her goal to visit every school in her conference, talking to the teachers, giving the students probably their first physical examination. A small area was set aside in the classroom for the examinations. She gave the children a hearing test. Using a long stick at one end she held a watch and asked if they could hear the clock ticking. Eyes were tested and she talked to them about personal hygiene, washing their hands correctly and overall cleanliness.

At the annual Union meeting held in Atlanta, she made a report of her work; she itemized every phase of her work and all correspondence. They were surprised at the volume of work that was accomplished and the detailed account that was presented. They asked her how she prepared the reports, she replied, "by hand of course." The committee was very impressed and Elder C.B. Stephenson, who was the Union President, suggested that a type-writer should be purchased and each conference would share in the expense. She was presented with a beautiful portable Corona typewriter. She was so pleased but now she had to learn how to type. Hunt and peck was a how she started, and before long she became good at typing. It was a good thing that it was portable because it became another part of her luggage and one more thing to carry as she traveled. She often worked while on the train and the typewriter was a big help to her.

Traveling from one city to another by train to cover all the churches and schools in the territory that was assigned to her was very hard at times. Her trunk and suitcase became her home away from home. She had very little cloths—her typical dress was a long black skirt with a tailored jacket, a crisp white blouse and a ribbon bow tie that she made by hand. In the summer months she would wear lighter colors such as a light blue, always with a blouse and bow tie.

She planned her work a month in advance and covered all the churches and schools in one Conference, before moving to another area. The trips generally took from six to eight weeks, but, by care-fully planning out her trips and taking advantage of various train routes she saved time and money.

The Florida trips were the longest because there were more

churches and mission schools to visit. The larger cities such as Atlanta, Jacksonville, Chattanooga, Nashville and Birmingham were visited often because she usually had to change trains in those cities. She took advantage of the time she visited those cities to get an update of the schools and churches and offer her assistance if needed. Her work among the colored people proved to be a great help to the Conferences. She was re-elected to the office with an additional responsibility of Educational Secretary in 1926.

Anna was so busy working that she did not have time to go home to Mississippi to visit her family. Grace wrote to her faithfully telling her about the garden she had planted and other goings on at the farm. This was a welcome diversion from all the strenuous work that she was doing. Of course she answered the letters and sometimes included a few dollars to help out. She was concerned about the health of her mother. Grace told her that she was getting a little frail and could not do much work on the farm anymore. Anna always answered their letters assuring them she would pray for the family to ask God to give them protection and comfort. A few months later she received a letter from her sister Grace telling her that their mother died on August 22, 1922. Their father (Newt) died in February, the same year. She left Atlanta for a few days to attend the funeral of her mother which was held graveside. She was buried in the Newton Knight Cemetery near Six Town. Anna returned to Atlanta and continued on with her work, more determined than ever to make sure the message reached all the colored people in her territory.

Chapter 13

The education Anna received at the Battle Creek Sanitarium, prepared her to work in the fertile mission field of the South. In an article she wrote as the Educational Secretary of the Southern Union Conference she stated:

"Many men and women were meeting the needs of the colored schools by educating the children. The hope of the race is for us to continue this noble work. Let us press onward and upward--educate, educate, educate head, heart and hand, until they have made a "New South." It can be done!

She wrote that the people in the cities and towns have taken old dilapidated log cabins and replaced them with neat school houses, barracks, tenement-houses and old shanties, which had been converted into splendid churches and schools. As a result, men and women and children who could scarcely spell, were being taught to read, write and to cipher, as well as being given trades and professions. Teachers had gone beyond their duties to go into the homes to teach healthful living, cooking, and first aid to the parents. The "New South" was beginning to take shape, although still segregated. The white superintendents of the conference were very helpful in assisting Anna to make the work a success.

Her work seemed to be a great help to the churches and schools. Of course she had a great responsibility that went with the position. She received help with the clerical work from the Union Conference Office staff. They wanted to provide an office for her, but she refused, believing strongly that her work was in the field and among the schools and churches. She had no time or need for an office. On her visits to different towns and cities, she not only met with the teachers, but participated in the church activities, such as Ingathering, Board Meetings, if invited and any other assistance that was needed.

On one of her trips she was traveling from Atlanta to Savannah, Georgia. She felt strong feeling that she needed to continue on to Charleston, South Carolina to visit one of the teachers. She reasoned with herself that it was not time to visit there yet and she must keep the itinerary as planned. She tried everything she could to get Charleston out of her mind, but felt she needed to continue on to Charleston. When she arrived at the train station in Savannah, she was met by the pastor of the church. She explained to him that she had to go to Charleston, and she would return the next day on the 2:00 PM train. She asked him to take her luggage to the place that she would be staying and to meet her the next day. Traveling to Charleston was troubling to her, because she could not understand why this teacher was on her mind. When she arrived and went to the school, the teacher met her with tears in her eyes and said:

> "Oh, Miss Knight, I am so glad you came! I wanted so much to see you, but couldn't write or telegraph because I did not know how to reach you. I need your help! So all I could do was to pray, which I did yesterday, and now you are here."

This was her first year of teaching and she needed some counsel and guidance. After providing her with the necessary instructions she requested, she return to her room. It was standard for the churches to provide a place for Anna to stay; the members gladly opened their home to her. She felt safe and comfortable staying with the families given that a woman traveling alone in different cities had to be careful.

As she was walking back to her room, she decided to call the train station to confirm her schedule. She looked around for a phone and noticed a pay phone in the funeral home. She asked the receptionist if she could use the phone. She called the station and was informed that her train was scheduled to leave an hour early. She hurriedly returned to her room, gathered her luggage and walked to the station just in time to catch the train to Savannah and continued her planned schedule. She was pleased that she took the time to visit the teacher to give her counsel and to let her know that she was doing a good job at the small church school and if she needed more help, to contact her.

Southern Union Conference

The Hope of the Race

Chapter 14

The work in the South among the colored people was progressing very well. New schools were opened, the churches were organized to carry out the mission work of the church, and young people were organized in the Missionary Volunteer Society. There was a great improvement in the education of the young people. She worked diligently within Southeastern Union Conference for six years. Both the Local Conference and the General Conference Officials were very pleased with the work that she did to improve the conditions among the colored race.

The Southeastern Union and the Southern Union Conferences merged to become the Southern Union Conference. The Southern Union Conference included the states of Louisiana, Mississippi, Alabama, western Florida, west Tennessee and Kentucky. They were in need of a person to again carry on the colored work for the new territory. At a meeting her name was brought up as the perfect person to handle the position since she was already doing the work, but on a smaller scale. She was approached by the Conference Officials and asked if she would consider the position as the Associate Secretary of Education, Young People's Missionary Society, and the Home Missionary Department of the colored area of the Southern Union. Anna had to really think about the new position, given that it would require her to do more traveling, and a substantial amount of record keeping. She asked them to give her a few days to think about it. She always spent time with God in prayer when she had a big decision to make. Her heart told her that she was needed and the people needed her most. There was not a person who had worked with the school and the churches before and she knew she had to accept the position.

She gave her answer to the Union Conference that she would take the position. They immediately placed a call to the General Conference asking for her release from the Southeastern Conference to accept the same position in the Southern Union Conference.

Before starting her work in her new position, Anna took the time to review and standardize the course of study, the textbooks, helped to select the right teachers, and improve the conditions of the schools under her leadership. She carefully prepared her itinerary so that she could cover as many cities and towns as possible along any given train route. In the churches she organized the members into groups for home missionary work and the youth group. She always paid special attention to the youth of the churches, because she wanted them to have the experience of worshiping in the church and to serve the community. To do all the work required she had to spend two days or even a week in each place.

There was an enormous amount of work to accomplish, with little money. Anna started a letter writing campaign to her friends. She also asked the churches to set aside one Sabbath a year to take a special offering in their church for their schools. She wrote to Mrs. Mary Foy, the Director of Nurses at The Battle Creek Sanitarium telling her about the work she had begun in the South in the colored department of the Union Conference asking for a contribution. Mrs. Foy read Anna's letter to the Alumni Association meeting and the members were very interested in her cause. Their funds were limited but they voted to send fifty dollars for the work and a note saying more would be coming. A few days later on February 5, 1931, she received a letter from the Secretary to Mr. W. K. Kellogg, Bessie Rogers. It read:

Dear Madam,

Mrs. Carrie Staines Kellogg has asked me to send you this enclosed Check for $200, which is to be used for the colored schools in the South.

Anna was pleased to receive the funds and to know that even though it was during the depression, people were inspired by the work being done for the colored department of our church organization and were still willing to help.

As a part of her responsibility for the colored work, she had to attend meetings at the Southern Union Office. Anna listened intently to the reports of the white department of the Southern Union. They had so many resources to pull from, and we had so little. At this one particular meeting of all the Conference Officials, Anna had to make her report. When it was her time to speak, she gave a detailed account of the work and made suggestions and requests for improvement. She was a person who was not afraid to tell the truth. She stood before the group and gave a speech after making her report:

"Permit me first of all to thank you for all you have done. For making it possible for me to attend the many meetings which I've attended. I hope I shall not be misunderstood by what I say here today.

But, as I sit here hour after hour and listen, I marvel. You have everything, we have so little. Colored people have always been an under privileged group. They are not inferior but under privileged.

In Mathew 15:21-28, Jesus said to Tyre and Sidon, a woman of Canaan from the coast came asking for help. She didn't give up; stood the test—Jesus rewarded her faith. This makes me think of our new group. And please may I ask that you continue to invite us to come to the table where we may get the crumbs.

Colored Youth need the same care as do the whites and more —much more. To strengthen our work, you must still hold the doors of the white Senior College and Sanitarium open to them. Don't segregate them where it is not necessary;

We should have all the regular activities at our Junior Camp and Senior camps, same as the whites; Once in a while representative groups of white and colored Workers should meet and discuss the local work frankly and sympathetically.

There should also be an exchange by experienced workers from Union to Union among the colored to visit our schools and churches;

Use "Mr. and Mrs." in writing letters. Don't be afraid to greet them. Don't tell stories about colored people in your Sermons to them.

Don't use the word 'you folk,' 'you people', or just 'folk' in your speaking to us, but, rather say—'Brethren' and 'Sisters.' Don't treat us like 'step children,' but as members of the family of God. If you can do these things, it will go a long way toward strengthening the work among the colored youth."

The Committee was stunned at her frankness. After the meeting some of the committee members approached her and thanked her for her work and showed concern for the colored people of the church.

She was glad to include in her report about the first Black Youth Congress held at Oakwood School for all the young people in the region--it was in 1934 on the campus of the Oakwood. There had never been a gathering of youth before in the church like that. Young people from all over the south attended the meeting. The members of the committee were impressed and left the meeting well educated on how to treat the colored race.

Her position as Associate Secretary of Education and Youth Department allowed her to be a member of the Board of Trustees at Oakwood Jr. College as it was known in 1922. During the summer months the Union Conference conducted summer school for all colored teachers. Anna taught Denomination History and Spirit of Prophecy. Mrs. R. A. Miller, a public school teacher of Savannah, Georgia attended the summer school. She was so impressed with the college that she thought the teachers should organize an association to better represent Christian education and to help the school and the students. The teachers in attendance became intensely interested in the work at Oakwood. Their hearts and minds were deeply stirred by a vison of the possibilities before the institution, and the need of better facilities to provide and care for the students who were in attendance and for others who should be encouraged to attend.

The teachers met together to consider a plan whereby they might do something to help Oakwood. After several meetings, the outcome was the organization of the National Colored Teachers Association, (NCTA). There were thirty-five teachers who joined as charter members. The officers elected were Anna Knight, President; Professor Frank L. Peterson, vice president; Julia F. Baugh, secretary-treasurer. Substantial pledges of money were raised during the school year of 1922-23.

Anna was the first and only president and she held that position until her death. The Association had many goals. Some of the goals accomplished included:

> Helped to provide a better water system at Oakwood Provided the first cement sidewalks on the campus of Oakwood Placed a large mirror in the hall in the girl's dormitory Created a student loan fund in 1923

Sarah E. Peck, then associate secretary of the General Conference Educational Department, gave the first one hundred dollars to establish the fund. Mrs. Miller gave $1000. The funds helped sixty-six students in the college. The NCTA was off to a good start. When others heard about the work that was being done, they willingly joined and supported the organization. This organization gave the teachers and administrators in education a platform to express and explore ideas in teaching.

Chapter 15

It was a rainy and chilly morning as she prepared to catch the train for Yazoo City, Mississippi. She was in a hurry, so there was no time for breakfast; only enough time to pack her trunk. The person who was assigned to get her to the train station was late. She was a little worried that she would not make the train in time because of the condition of the roads and the rainy weather. When she arrived at the station to purchase her ticket, the agent would not sell her the ticket she needed on the discounted clergy permit. She had to purchase a ticket for the full price because she had to reach her next destination on time. As she boarded the train, and settled into a comfortable seat she looked out the window and noticed that the train was not moving. Other trains left but her train was still at the station. After it finally left, the conductor came through the aisle and began to collect the tickets. He noticed her ticket immediately and said: Madam you are on the wrong train."

He pulled the cord to stop the train. Anna and two other ladies had to get off the train about a mile from the train station in the middle of the wet, muddy road in the delta. They had to walk back to the train station carrying their hand luggage and try to make arrangements to catch the right train. The station was crowded because of the storm and trains were running late. She looked at the crowd of people waiting for trains and thought if she was going to make her next appointment on time, she had to find another way to Yazoo City. The two ladies who walked back to the train station with Anna seemed to be upset. They too, were anxious to continue on with their trip. She did not know the ladies but they seemed to be friendly, so Anna asked if they would share a taxi with her to take them from Morehead to Yazoo City which was about sixty miles, they agreed. Anna left her typewriter and suitcase with them as she ventured into the town to find a taxi. All of the taxies were taken. As she looked down the muddy street, she saw a white man standing beside his car. Anna needed to continue her trip and there was no other way but to ask the man if his car was for hire. Luckily he was for hire and agreed to take them to Yazoo City for twelve dollars. When she arrived back to the station she told the ladies that she had found someone that would drive them and that it would be four dollars each. They agreed and started out on their journey. The car was an old car with worn tires. Anna didn't know the condition of the car and prayed all the time that they did not make the wrong decision. Before they could go very far, they had a flat tire; everyone exited the car so he could repair the flat tire. While waiting they noticed that all the tires on the car were worn. But they had already started on the trip and had no other choice but to continue with him.

The roads were bad and they did not get very far before they had another flat tire. The ladies were frustrated, but they did not blame Anna for the decision they made to have the man take them to Yazoo City. As their driver fixed the second flat tire, Anna discovered that her purse was missing. She looked inside the car and asked the ladies if they had seen her purse.

"No, you must have left it at the station." The lady said.

"I had important papers, my fountain pen, clergy permit, and $5 in change in it," Anna replied.

The ladies were a little stunned at her reaction and helped her to look for it in the car again. She asked the man to take her back to the train station because she must have left her handbag there. Again the two ladies were left on the side of the highway as Anna and the driver returned to the train station. The driver has so many flats that he finally asked Anna to ride with someone else who could take her back to the station and he would meet her there to take her back to the ladies waiting on the highway. When she arrived at the train station the people were surprised to see her and asked why she came back?

Anna replied: "I am looking for my handbag, it is black with a short handle, have you seen it?"

"No", they replied.

She searched the waiting room, asking other passenger if they had found a handbag. A few of the passengers helped her to look, but the handbag was not there. After about an hour of searching for the handbag, Anna came to the conclusion that it was lost or someone had taken it. There was no other choice but to continue on without the papers and her permit and no money. She prayed again that the Lord would provide for her. Finally, the driver returned and took her back to the ladies who were waiting along the highway. By this time they were very impatient as they started out on their trip again. The driver complained all the way about the bad roads and how much it cost him to get his tires repaired. Anna and the ladies were very perturbed for fear they would not reach their destination. They noticed that the driver was asking several people directions to Yazoo City. He had told them that he knew the way when they engaged his services. Either he was a crook or he really did not know how to get to Yazoo City. After a long and tiresome ride, and much prayer, they finally reached Yazoo city. Anna thanked the ladies for their patience and understanding and everyone went on their way.

Anna had never been to Yazoo City before. A meeting had

been planned for that evening and she was to speak. The local elder of the church was to meet her at the station to take her to the church. Because she was late arriving the local elder that was to meet her at the train was not there. Anna had $1.00 in her jacket pocket, so she got it changed and obtained a locker to store her luggage. First, she prayed and thanked the Lord for bringing her to the city safely, and asked to help her find the church. She started out walking and asked a local gentleman who was coming down the street toward her if he knew any Seventh-day Adventists in town.

"Yes," he said. "See that house up there on the corner? One of them lives there."

Anna thanked him and went to the house, but no one was home. She sat on the porch because she was so tired from the trip and frustrated because she lost her purse and credentials. After a little while, a man rode by on a horse and stopped at the gate.

"Are you Anna Knight?" he asked.

"Yes," she replied.

"I came to the train station to meet you but you were not on it. I did not know if you were coming or not so I told the people we would not have the meeting tonight. They were really excited about coming to hear you speak," he said.

Anna told him about the trouble she had trying to reach Yazoo City to keep her appointment. She asked if he could contact the people and explain to them what happened and that there will be a meeting after all. He contacted as many people as he could, explained to them what happened and to come back to the church that Miss Knight will be there to speak. He told Anna to tell the first person who reached the church to turn on the lights and the people will come. That meeting was a very good meeting, and about fifteen or twenty people attended. As usual, the people were spellbound listening to her talk about all of her work in India.

They especially enjoyed hearing about how she started the school in Gitano. After her talk, she lingered a little longer because the people wanted to ask questions about her work as well as what they could expect from the Union Conference. She told them that she could not do all the work of spreading the gospel alone, they must also help.

Anna also told the people what had happened on her trip to Yazoo City, and that she did not have any money to reach Jackson Mississippi where she could get a loan from the Conference to take her to Nashville. They were very happy to give her the money needed so she could reach her next destination. It was a lesson well learned for Anna—never start out your day without having a word with God first. After a good night's sleep, she continued on her journey to Nashville, Tennessee.

She spent a few days in Nashville before traveling to her home in Chattanooga. Anna completed her reports and went to the Union Conference office to submit them. In spite of all the obstacles that she faced on the trip, she was able to give a good report. All the schools were doing well, teachers' concerns had been met and churches continued to gain new members.

Anna's travels throughout the south took her to cities and towns where she visited many of the churches and schools. She felt guilty that she did not have very much time to visit with her family back home in Mississippi. Grace, her sister, kept in touch with her writing letters to let her know what was going on at home. Often times she would ask Anna for money to help buy equipment or other items to keep up the farm. At that time Grace had two nephews living with her. They were a good help with the farm work even though they were young.

Before starting out on another trip she told the officials that she would go by her home in Six Town for a few days and then continue on to her next appointment. It was good for her to see her relatives. She visited the Soso Church where she always sent her tithe, and talked with the group of worshipers. People from all over the community came to hear her speak about her experiences and how the Union Conference was supporting the colored work. Anna was glad that the small church in Soso was going well. They had about thirty to forty members. John "Henchie" Knight, her uncle, was the head deacon, and Floyd Booth was the head elder. Together they were good leaders of the church. The first pastor of the church was C.B. Holloway, a Bible worker in Laurel who walked the railroad tracks from Laurel to Soso every Saturday morning to conduct churches services. After a few days of rest and good country food, Anna continued on with her trip. This time she was scheduled to go back to Jackson to meet with the people there and visit the school.

She thought that since it was going to be a short trip there was no need to take a lunch. Her faithful brother Howard took her to the train station in Laurel by horse and buggy. It was a cloudy day and looked like rain, but it was not raining at the time. As she boarded the train and took her seat, she waved good bye to her brother and prayed that he would have safe travels back to Six Town. The train had to travel through Mendenhall to reach Jackson. When they were three miles from Mendenhall it began to rain and thunder and lightning, the train was rocking from side to side on the tracks. The conductor ordered the train to stop on the tracks before continuing on to the next station which was Braxton, Mississippi. What she did not know was that a tornado had struck the town of Braxton and the train tracks were underwater. They could not go any further. Everyone was ordered off the train and they were left to find places to stay until the storm subsided. The train was sidetracked in Delo; the conductor gave the passengers back their tickets and told them they had to make other arrangements. Anna did not know anyone and asked if she could stay on the train. Her request was granted but at her own risk. There were five men left on the train including the porter. With no food or water and a train full of men, this was one time Anna prayed all night because she was the only women on the train. Anna made sure that her handbag was safe before she fell asleep. She was thankful that the conductor had stopped the train and saved her life as well as others. At daybreak the train tracks were safe enough to continue to the next station. They were allowed to leave the train to find something to eat. As she got off the train she looked around at all the devastation that the storm had caused. The water in the well was muddy from the heavy rain, stores were not open. There was not a place that had food or water. She had to continue on relying on her faith to get her through the journey.

About mid-morning the conductor announced that the tracks were clear enough for them to continue on. Anna was so thankful to continue to her destination, but she was very hungry and thirsty. When she arrived at the station in Jackson, she was met by the husband of the family that she was going to stay with. The first thing she asked him was, "Where can I get something to eat." She explained to him the problems that the train had trying to get through the tornado area and that she did not bring a lunch. He put his arms around her shoulders and said:

"Don't worry Miss Knight, my wife has prepared a special meal for you," he said.

Anna gave a sigh of relief. Once again someone was looking out for her. When she arrived at the home of the family, she was greeted with warm smile and was immediately shown to her room. Anna could smell the aroma of the food coming from the kitchen, she could not wait until dinner was ready and to eat the delicious food that had been prepared for her. As soon as she was settled in her room, she went to the dining room; the table was set with a tablecloth, beautiful china and silverware, and bowls of food just waiting to be devoured. After enjoying the meal she sat with her guest host to talk for a while over dessert. Retiring to her room for a good night sleep, she thought about the events that had happen that day. Thankful that she had survived the storm safely her eyes closed and she rested peacefully through the night knowing that she was safe. The next morning there was no rain and the sun was shining bright. Her host prepared a delicious breakfast and told her to go about her work and dinner would be ready when she returns home.

Anna visited to the schools in the area and met with the pastors of the churches to see how the work was progressing and if they needed any assistance. It was a busy two days in Jackson but she was happy that she had a comfortable place to stay and did not have to worry about her meals.

Chapter 16

Anna was returning from a very busy and long trip visiting all the schools and churches in the Southeastern states that were in the Southern Union. Birmingham, Alabama was a hub for trains in the South and this is where she often spent the night with the Blaylock family. On this particular trip she had planned to take the morning train to Huntsville to attend a meeting at Oakwood School. As fate would have it, there was a heavy rain during the night that continued into the early morning. The train was delayed until the tracks were inspected and it was safe to travel.

Because of her work schedule, there was little time for her to shop for herself, and she needed a pair of shoes. She asked the husband of the lady that she was staying with to take her to the shoe store. He agreed under the condition that she had to get ready quickly. Anna thought there was no way that she could pack her suitcase, grab a bite to eat and be ready to go within fifteen minutes. She told him to go ahead and leave without her. Silently she prayed that God would make a way somehow. She looked out the window and saw that it was still raining. She did not know who could take her to the train station and a shoe store before the train was scheduled to leave. Anna thanked her hostess and approached the door to leave. To her surprise her hostess's husband who was to take her to station, was stuck in mud in the yard. His was trying desperately to get the car out. He laughed at himself.

"Come on, I'll take you to town."

She reminded him that she wanted to go to the shoe store first before going to the train station. "You had better go to the train station first to make sure that the train is on time." Upon arriving at the train station, she was informed that the train would be twenty-five minutes late.

"We will have just enough time to go to the store if we hurry," she said. She bought her ticket as he suggested, checked her luggage and they went searching for the nearest shoe store. " "Get in. It's your risk, not mine" he said with a smile.

The train station was located in downtown Birmingham and the stores were nearby. It looked as if the rain was never going to stop long enough for her to make her purchase of the shoes. She carried her umbrella with her at all times and she made good use of it that day. They looked for a few minutes and found a store that carried the shoes that she was looking for. She found a clerk to assist her. She asked:

"Sir I am looking for a pair of shoes, just like the ones I have on."

"I only have one pair like that and I don't know if they are your size" the clerk replied.

"Bring them and let me try them on."

As Anna put her foot into the shoes, she smiled. "These are a perfect fit."

The only problem was they cost about $12, and that was a lot of money to pay for a pair of shoes, especially when the country was in a depression. With the limited funds that Anna had, she did not want to spend that much for the shoes, but she needed a pair of shoes. However, there was little time left to do more comparison shopping, so she purchased the shoes.

With her new shoes under her arm she returned to the train station. She was glad that she had purchased her ticket and checked her luggage earlier, because the porter was calling for people to board the L & N train to Huntsville. As she took her seat she was still worried because the train was twenty-five minutes late. It might not be enough time for her to make the Southern train which was the connecting train in Decatur, Alabama. If she missed the Southern train, then there was a five hour wait until the next train arrived at the Huntsville station. It would mean that she would arrive in Huntsville late in the evening, and she did not know if there will be anyone there to pick her up. Fortunately, she did make her connecting train in Decatur. The porter took her luggage and ticket, and she boarded the train just in time. She took a deep breath and thanked the Lord. One of the other passengers responded, "You need not thank the Lord, you need to thank the freight train that blocked the tracks." She and the other passengers had a good laugh, but she said, "I thank Him anyway."

As the train was making its way to Huntsville, the skies were beginning to clear and the rain stopped. The rocking sounds of the train caused Anna to relax and take a much needed nap for a little while. When she heard the porter call out "Huntsville Alabama," next stop, she began to gather her luggage and make her way to the front of the train. Anna exited the train and proceeded to the waiting room. She did not know if anyone would be there to meet her. To her surprise there was Brother Dobbins from Oakwood College standing on the platform. He was just as surprised to see her.

"How did you know that I was coming?" Anna asked.

"I didn't," he said. "But I was in town and felt the need to come by the station to see if anyone needed a ride to the campus." Mr. Dobbins replied.

"God works in mysterious ways," she said.

As Anna and Mr. Dobbins were driving to the Oakwood campus which was about seven miles from Huntsville, her mind wandered back to the time she heard Sister Ellen White and others talking about a site for a school for the colored people. At the time she was living with Mr. Dyo Chambers and his wife in Chattanooga, Tennessee. They had stopped by to visit and to consult with the Chambers about the farm that they had located in Huntsville, Alabama.

Anna listened as Ellen White and the other individuals traveling with her pray earnestly that this would be the right place for a school. The feeling of racial tension would not be as bad in the northern section of Alabama as in the deep southern part. It was very important that whatever place it was located that it had to be safe for the colored students to study and live in peace. After arriving on the campus and seeing the progress that had been made, Anna thought about all the sacrifices that had been made in order to purchase the Oakwood School. To see it now, with both young women and men attending classes and working their way through school, warmed her heart. Oakwood, however, was still a farm and they grew much of their own fruit and vegetables. The school had a dairy that provided milk for the school cafeteria as well as stores in Huntsville.

On this trip to Oakwood College she was attending a Board Meeting. Elder Tucker was president of the College. Being a part of the Board to help plan the growth of the College gave her great satisfaction. The school had grown from Oakwood School, Oakwood Junior College, Oakwood College and now Oakwood University. Many of the ministers, teachers and nurses received their training at Oakwood and went on to become successful pastors, teachers and nurses throughout the United States and other foreign countries. As she took a walk around the campus she could see growth that had taken place. New dormitories had been built to house the young ladies and young men. The campus was beautiful and beginning to take shape into a circle surrounded by tall oak trees. Beautiful flower beds had been planted and this caught the eye of Anna. Seeing the farm on Oakwood's Campus, reminded her of her family farm in Mississippi where she grew up. This indeed was "The Place Where Loveliness Keeps House."

After the Board meeting, she returned to Chattanooga for a few weeks of rest and to make all the necessary reports to the Union Conference on the progress of the Colored Union Department. In her reports she noted that during her years of service, thirty-four church schools were established, four of which were junior academies; fifty-four teachers were employed and the schools were doing well. But, as always, there was still more work to be done in the colored department of the church. It would always be an ongoing process and someone had to continue the work after she was gone.

It felt good to her to be in her home in Chattanooga sleeping in her own bed, even if it was a one room in someone's home. There was little time for vacation during her years of work. A two week vacation with pay was allowed in her work schedule, but she did not take it. There was always so much work to be done and Anna felt that she was the one called to do it.

On one occasion while attending a camp meeting in Florida, she was invited to Nassau Bahamas to take a vacation by the delegation that was also attending the meeting. All the expenses would be paid; all she had to do was arrange her schedule to attend. She decided to take them up on their offer and plan a much needed vacation. Elder and Mrs. D.B. Reid were returning to Nassau where they were working in the mission field there. They traveled to the island of the Bahamas on a small boat, called "The Champion". They left on December 26, 1937 and arrived in Nassau in the midafternoon the next day. The boat ride over to the island of Nassau was a little rough, but she did not get seasick. The weather was warm with a slight breeze blowing. It was a beautiful tropical island with colorful flowers and trees. To her surprise a large number of people were at the dock to meet them. Among them was a student she had met at Oakwood years before who was a self-supporting missionary nurse named Miss Woods. She was very pleased to be invited to stay in her home while visiting the island. Although it was supposed to be a vacation, there were quite a few speaking engagements lined up for her. Not all of it was work. The members were very excited and proud to show her their island. Taking a street car to visit all the tourist attractions was very enjoyable to Anna. In fact, she enjoyed her stay so much that she had her ticket extended to stay a few days longer. The food was delicious, especially all the tropical fruits. The mangos tasted almost like the mangos that she was so fond of in East India. There were two large churches in the city of Nassau and Anna was invited to speak at both of them. To her the memory of that visit to Nassau would always be etched in her mind, even if it was a working vacation. She enjoyed it because the people were friendly and went out of their way to make sure that she was comfortable. On January 9th, 1938 she left the island to return to Chattanooga to continue her work.

Anna had worked tirelessly among the black people trying to see that they had the same opportunities for education and healthful living as the white people. She was a very determined lady. She stood and fought for the rights of the less fortunate. This seemed to be her life's work, like when she had to fight off the moonshiners in her home state of Mississippi so they couldn't interfere in the education of the people who were less fortunate. It was her calling and it was a cause she was determined to accomplish, and she did.

Retirement Years

Chapter 17

Since Anna had spent most of her life traveling and living on the train and suitcases, she felt that it was time for her to retire from her work. She wrote a letter to the Southern Union and told them she wanted to retire. She asked that they find someone younger to oversee the Colored Department of the Conference. She also was looking for a place to put down her final roots and to live out the rest of her life. In December 1945 the black conferences were organized and the black Southern Union Department was automatically dissolved as well as her position as Associate Secretary of several departments within the Southern Union. By then she had reached the age of seventy-two and wanted to live a stress free life with comfortable surroundings. She wrote a letter to Oakwood College in Huntsville, Alabama and expressed to them that she was going to retire and wanted to know if she could live on the campus. They responded immediately stating they would be pleased to have her as a permanent resident of the Oakwood family.

Before she made her move to retire, she went to spend time with her sister Grace and her nephews in Mississippi. The farm was left to Grace, Anna and Lassie by their mother in her will. Their brother Howard had already received his portion when he became of age and married. Grace stayed on the farm and was taking care of her two nephews, Cecil and Hillman. Lassie had moved to Texas. Anna enjoyed visiting with all the family members and visiting the Soso Church, which was her home Church. The Church had her speak about all her work in the Mission Fields of India and the Mission Field the Black departments of the conference. Every year she returned and gave all the students at the Soso School physical examinations, just as she had done with all the black schools. She also encouraged members to participate in the church and continue to educate the children. Anna faithfully continued to send her tithe to the Soso Church, because there were so few members and the tithes and offerings would help the Church. Whenever possible she included a little extra money to help with the upkeep and other expenses.

After a few weeks, Anna returned to Chattanooga to make preparation for her move to Oakwood College, which was to be her retirement home. Grace made sure that Anna returned with plenty of canned fruits and vegetables and peanuts that she loved. She also told Grace that now that she was not traveling so much, she could visit more often. Grace was very happy about that and proceeded to make arrangements for Anna's transportation to the train station in Ellisville. Grace asked a relative to take them in their car. As they were riding the narrow dirt roads, Anna was looking out the window smelling the fresh hay that had just been cut. She looked over the farms that were neatly laid out in rows, ready to be harvested and marveled at the tall pine trees. It reminded her of the times she had to ride her horse through the tall pine trees trying to get away from the moonshiners who were chasing her for teaching against drinking. She and Grace were remembering the days in their early childhood when she had to plow the fields on her mother's land to plant the crops. Even though she did not appreciate the hard work then, it taught her to be very determined in all of her work and to make sure to complete each task given to her. Arriving at the train station with time to spare, Anna purchased her ticket for Chattanooga. She lingered a little longer with her sister and nephew. The train finally arrived from New Orleans, Louisiana and was partially full. She was able to find a seat by the window. Her sister Grace and nephews Hillman and Cecil stood on the platform waving goodbye as the train slowly started to move. Anna could not help but to shed a few tears, but this time they were tears of joy knowing that she was going to have more time to spend with her family in Mississippi. Traveling back was bringing memories of her many miles of travel throughout all the cities she had visited, sometimes making stops in towns where she did not know anyone. God was always with her to guide her and keep her on a safe and comfortable path.

It was a cool, cloudy morning when the train arrived in Chattanooga the next morning. Anna took a taxi to her home. As the driver traveled down the streets she was looking out the window admiring the beautiful red and gold leaves on the trees that lined the streets. She was very tired from traveling and was anxious to get to her room. After settling in her room and looking over her mail, she noticed a letter from Oakwood College. In it they informed her that they had found a place for her to live on the campus. Henderson Hall, the academy girls' dormitory was to be her new home. This was pleasing to her because she was to have a room and cooking privileges if she wanted. She especially enjoyed the fact that she would be around young people. After a few days of rest, she began packing. There was no furniture to be moved because she spent most of her adult life traveling and living out of her suitcase and trunk. The next few days she took her time to pack her suitcases, trunk and boxes. Sorting through all the papers and deciding what to keep and what should be thrown away was her biggest challenge. Finally the packing was complete and she was ready to move to Oakwood. She called the taxi to take her to the train station. The driver loaded his car with her luggage and boxes took her to the station. After all the train rides that she had taken, this will be the best one, the train to Huntsville, Alabama. This was in the fall of 1951 and Oakwood College became her permanent home.

She was met at the Huntsville station by a representative of the College. Arriving on the campus of Oakwood brought joy to her heart. She was greeted by Trula Wade, the dean of Henderson Hall academy girls' dormitory. Miss Wade showed Anna her room which was across the hall from her apartment. Anna made her living quarters homey and comfortable, just like she wanted. Miss Wade and Anna became close friends. In fact Miss Wade became her assistant and they eventually shared a house together. Now that she had more time on her hands, she could some of the things that she loved, such as planting flowers around the campus. Several people encouraged Anna to write an autobiography about her life. Although she thought that everyone knew about her, she finally decided to write *Mississippi Girl*. It was published in 1952.

Anna did most of her corresponding by letter given that she had beautiful penmanship. Miss Wade sometime read letters to her when her eyesight was fading. She kept a record of each letter and card received, recording the date when and if she answered them. Anna continued to serve as the President of the National Colored Teachers' Association and faithfully sent out newsletters to all the members.

From her mother, Anna developed a love for flowers. Working in the flower beds on the campus was her favorite past time. Her fondness for beautiful flowers was shown in the way that she cared and cultivated the flower beds near the President's house and Henderson Hall. She did not think twice about asking anyone that was walking by on their way to class or work to take a minute to help her. Sometimes she gave them twenty-five cents, but most times the students were happy to help her. She had a special seat in Moran Hall, the building where the church, vesper and chapel services were held. Classes were also held in Moran Hall. Everyone on the campus knew about her special seat in the auditorium except for the new students. The students waited for the new person to sit in her seat which was the first seat on the second row on the girl's side of the auditorium. They could not wait to see the reaction when she approached them and tapped them on the shoulder with her umbrella or gave them a stern look, and said: "Don't you know you are sitting in my seat?" All of the other students laughed and got a kick out of seeing this happen time after time.

On Wednesday night in the dorms, chapel was held. Anna looked forward to attending and seeing all the young ladies of Henderson Hall. She enjoyed speaking in front of the group of young ladies, recounting her experience in the mission field of India as well as other pioneers who worked tirelessly. The residents of Henderson Hall listened eagerly to her many experiences, and as one of them said, "It is an honor to have you with us Miss Knight." Anna's birthday was March 4th and at that particular chapel meeting the young ladies wanted to do something special for her and a good friend, Mrs. Bessie Peterson, who was the President's wife. Both shared the same birthday. The young ladies solicited funds from other dorms and faculty members to purchase gifts for the two deserving women whom they admired so much. The gifts were presented at the regular chapel meeting by a senior Carolyn Thompson and freshmen Francis Christian. Along with the gifts, they read a verse from the following poem as a tribute to her:

The Inaugural Child

About 70 years ago, might be less or more
A sweet little girl was born on March four.

Now this little girl grew up in a large family of poverty
But, amid all this she was as happy as a child could be

She didn't have the opportunity to go to school,
She was determined with all her might
That come what may, she would learn to read and write

Anna smiled as she received the gift and listened to the poem written about her. It made her feel appreciated and she felt that all the work she had done over the years was clearly worthwhile. She could see it in the way the young ladies at the college acted with such charm and grace.

Her retirement years were not used to sit and do nothing. Besides working on the campus with her flower ministry, she continued to serve as the president of the National Colored Teachers Association. She faithfully sent out newsletters to the members keeping them abreast of all the news regarding education. Future Adventist leaders and teachers often came to her seeking counsel as well as the young students on the campus.

Every year at Christmas, Anna traveled to her sister Grace's home in Mississippi to spend the holidays with her and her nephews Cecil and Hillman. This was an enjoyable time and Anna also had a chance to visit other family members and to attend her Church in Soso. Family members loved to visit her at Grace's and wanted to hear about her experiences each time they came. As much as she enjoyed spending time with family members it was always good to return back to her home at Oakwood College. By this time a new dean was hired for Henderson Hall. Anna her friend Trula Wade moved to a house on the campus. It was a neat small house furnished very nicely and comfortable. Of course Anna planted flowers in front of the house which gave her something to do.

Anna had reached a great milestone in her life when she turned ninety years old on March 4th, 1964. The National Chapter of the Oakwood College Alumni Association planned a Birthday Testimonial in her honor. It was called, "Miss Anna Knight, This Is Your Life." The evening was filled with remarks, music and fun from all of her friends and students. Then to top off the evening, she was presented with a beautiful reclining rocking chair. For Anna, it was the best present of all, and she used it well during her retirement. You could find her sitting by the window in the recliner looking over the beautiful campus of Oakwood and watching the students as they were going to and from their classes. She was very content with her life on the campus of Oakwood College. She was a woman of purpose and determination…and in her mature years, her support and dedication had wrought great things for the cause she lived for.…..Education.

Another honor was presented to her by The General Conference Department of Education. Anna was awarded the Medallion of Merit, in recognition of extraordinary and meritorious service to Christian Education. It is the highest recognition given by the General Conference of Seventh-day Adventist. The award was presented to her by Dr. Charles Hirsch, Secretary for the General Conference on November 17, 1971 at Oakwood College. She was the thirteenth person to receive the Medallion of Merit. Anna was both delighted and appreciative of this Award presented to her and in her acceptance speech she said, "I hope that others will continue to further the cause of education. It is much easier now, then, when I started. My work and my life show how much can be done with so little; Faith, Trust and Patience are the key."

Final Chapter

Chapter 18

Anna constantly worried about her family in Mississippi; her sister Grace, her nephews Cecil and Hillman, who were living on the farm in the family house in Six Town. She kept in touch with her sister by writing letters to her to see how she was doing and how the other family members were doing.

Grace and her nephews continued to farm, they seemed to be doing very well with their gardens of vegetables, peas, butterbeans and Anna's favorite, peanuts. They had a few cows, six calves, a bull, and chickens. Grace made fresh butter using milk from the cows and sold it. She typically would earn about three dollars a week. Bushels of peas and butterbeans were also sold to people in the community or given to family members. It was the custom in their community to take care of any family member first who may need food or, share with others. When it was harvest time, they gathered all the fruits and vegetables and prepared them for canning, made jelly and jam from the fruit, so there would be plenty of food for them in the winter. There was no freezing at the time, because most did not have refrigerators. The ladies enjoyed going around to each other's houses to see what they had canned for the season. Everyone was proud to show off the canned goods. Grace canned extra vegetables, jellies and peanuts to send to Anna whenever she heard of anyone going to Oakwood.

Anna was always excited to read Grace's letters. She gave an account of how she spent her day. Every time she read her letters she longed to be there with Grace and the rest of the family, but her calling and work was at Oakwood. Grace kept Anna up to date on all the happenings in the family and the church. Grace told her on Sabbath mornings on her way to the church in Soso in her horse and buggy, she picked up as many children that could fit in her buggy and took them to Sabbath School. The children and adults stood on the side of the road waiting for her as she traveled along the red clay dirt road from Six Town community to Soso each Saturday morning. This news brought a big smile to Anna's face, she knew her sister Grace was the pianist for the church and everyone in the church, mostly family members, participated in one way or another, sometimes even delivering the sermon.

After a while, the letters received from Grace were about her health; shortness of breath and high blood pressure. Anna being the older sister cautioned her about doing too much work on the farm, admonishing her to eat right and drink lots of water. Gracie assured her that Hillman and Cecil were doing most of the work and she was mainly taking care of the house. Of course, Anna knew that this was not so, but what could she do being so far away? Whenever she could spare extra money, Anna sent it to Grace to help purchase a tractor and other farm equipment to make farming easier. The farm was sort of general store for the community, supplying milk, butter, vegetables, melons and eggs. Aunt Hilda and her daughter Annette, and her aunt Idell frequently visited Grace. Sometimes Grace read the letters she received from Anna to them. Everyone enjoyed hearing them and was glad she was doing well. Receiving letters from other family members kept Anna informed of the family in Mississippi. As Anna's eyesight was failing, Trula Wade, Anna's friend, read the letters to her. She smiled with satisfaction hearing all the goings and comings of her family.

Anna could tell by the tone of Grace's letters that her health was beginning to deteriorate. Her handwriting was getting weaker, so Hillman began to write for her. Cecil did not correspond very much with Anna, because he felt that his aunt Grace cared more about Hillman than him. In one of her letters Grace told Anna that Hillman was having problems with his kidney and had to be rushed to the Community Hospital in Laurel. Anna became very concerned about her family and prayed that God would take care of them. Dr. Applewhite, who was their doctor, called in a kidney specialist to examine Hillman. He stayed in the hospital for two days then was released and given instructions to take it easy for a while and not do any heavy lifting or anything. Since Hillman was Grace's right hand, she was at a loss as to how she was going to manage all the work that had to be done on the little farm. She had hoped that she could depend on Cecil to help more. No matter how hard she tried with Cecil, he was still not interested in farm work; instead he was interested in leaving and moving to the big city.

As time went on, Anna and Grace both were getting sick and they told each other about their ailments. In Anna's letters she included magazines and pamphlets in hopes that it would cheer her up. Family members all pitched in to help Grace. Her uncle Lacy and aunt Idell came over every evening to help with the cows and other chores. Annette took them to the doctor to refill their prescriptions. Uncle Ernest and aunt Vilenda brought food already cooked for their dinner. As with any large and close knit family, they were a great help to Anna's sister and her nephews, but they also had homes and farms to attend to. Anna's heart was aching because she wanted to be with her sister to help out. Each time she received a letter from Grace, she hoped that she would say that she was getting better, but that was not the case. Anna sent money to help pay the hospital and doctors' bills. Cecil had decided that the farm life was not for him. He wanted a little more excitement in his life and to make money on his own. He left the farm and moved to Natchez, Mississippi, feeling that his aunt Grace would not miss him because she had Hillman who was her favorite. But she loved both of her nephews the same. In a letter to Anna, Cecil told her that he had a good job making ninety-five dollars per week. That was good money in those days, so he had bought a Cadillac for $1,100. He said he was living the good life and that he did not miss the farm life in Six Town. This brought tears to Anna's eyes. She prayed for her sister and nephews constantly but there was nothing more that she could do. Anna confided in her friend Trula Wade about her concerns for the family in Mississippi. Ms. Wade assured her that God would take care of her family and she should stop worrying so much and to make sure that she took care of herself because she was getting up in age. Anna appreciated the concern that Ms. Wade had for her and tried to stop worrying so much. She just has to put everything in the hands of God.

As she continued to enjoy her retirement years at Oakwood, many honors were bestowed on her for all the work she did to further the Black work among the Adventist Church, and the Mission Field. Most of all for the work in making sure that every black child who wanted could get an education. She stayed in contact with her many friends. Most of her days were spent corresponding with people who wanted her advice on issues or just to stay in contact. She was still the president of the National Colored Teachers Association and continued to write and send out the newsletters to the members. The members looked forward to receiving the newsletters, especially the one around Christmas time. It was always filled with good cheer and all the events that had happed that year. Her life was a busy one, as she sat meditating over the great world-wide work; her heart was filled with joy to know that she played a small part in the progress that had been made with her people.

In October, 1966, Anna received word that her beloved sister Grace had died. She was seventy-five years old. Even though she knew that her sister was very sick, still the shock of her death deeply affected Anna. As she prepared to travel to Six Town to make the funeral arrangements for her sister, she could not fight back the tears. She just sat down and had a good cry. Arriving in Ellisville, Hillman met her at the station and drove her back home to Six Town. The funeral was held at Grace's home church in Soso. Lessie, their sister came home from Texas to attend the funeral. Anna was glad to see her sister even on this sad occasion. Grace had a small insurance policy to help cover some of the expenses, and Anna paid the balance of the cost to bury their sister. The Soso SDA Church was filled with family members, members of the church and friends from the community. She was buried in the family cemetery near Six Town, the same place where their father Newton Knight is buried.

Grace left a will, leaving everything to her nephews Hillman and Cecil. Anna was the administrator. It was not long before Hillman who was thirty years old at the time, ignored the will and began to sell everything, the cattle, timber, all the farm equipment and did not share anything with his brother Cecil. After Hillman sold what he could, he moved to New Jersey, Cecil remained in Natchez. There was nothing left of the farm but the land so Anna made arrangements to sell the land. It was very painful for Anna the way everything was done, but she wiped her tears and moved ahead. She kept in touch with them when they answered her letters, after all, they were her family and she never stopped praying and caring for them. Anna remained at Oakwood and tried to put the past behind her. She continued to counsel and inspire others but never forgot about her family.

Anna's own health was becoming a concern; she went to see her Doctor at the Riverside Hospital in Nashville, Tennessee for an examination. The Doctor thought it was best to admit her. Because of her age, they wanted to keep her for a few days to monitor her condition. After a few days, her long and useful life ended at the age of ninety-eight on June 3, 1972, severing a link to the past that cannot be replaced.

The news of her death spread throughout the Adventist Community, many hearts were sad. The world had lost a great woman who did not walk in the cast off shoes of others, but on her own path that she created. The people whose lives she had touched attended her funeral held in Moran Hall on the campus of Oakwood College. Many kind words were spoken about her by the General and Local Conference Officials and others for her dedication to Seventh-day Adventist education...

Life was full of excitement for Anna Knight, a woman of purpose and determination. She made life better for others following in her footsteps. This woman of courage from the Deep South of Mississippi left legacies that all who believe in serving and educating others should strive to do so. Since 1911, Anna kept a detailed record of her work; she conducted 9,388 meetings, made 11,744 missionary visits, wrote 48,918 letters and traveled 554,439 miles, which did not include miles traveled in India. Yes, you can say she was happy.

Her final request was to be taken back to Six Town to be buried in the Knight Family cemetery where her father, mother and sister are resting in peace. Anna Knight's request was granted and her body was taken back to Six Town, Mississippi resting on a hill among the tall pine trees. With no headstone just a simple sign with her name and birth date and date of death. She is the last person to be buried in the *Newt Knight Family Cemetery*. Although her long and busy life has ended, her memory and legacy continue to live through this book and people she has touched with words, wisdom and works.

As she wrote in her book, *Mississippi Girl*:

> *"Now that I have come to the sunset hours of my active work and the close of this little story, I am indeed happy as I look back over the years to see the way the Lord has ruled and overruled in the things pertaining to my life and work. There is only one regret, and that is that I could not do more. My life has been a busy one; Hands and Hearts have been full. When I look at the scores of young men and women whom I met first in our mission and church school and encouraged and assisted, I sit here meditating over the great worldwide work. My heart is filled to overflowing with gratitude to God. To see young people get a Christian education, and to see them out in the field filling places of responsibility and trust. Bearing heavy burdens in our institutions, serving as evangelist, teachers, doctors, nurses, Bible instructors, bookkeepers, secretaries, and executives. Am I happy? Oh, yes, I am happy!"*

The Legacy Continues

Chapter 19

⌒⌒

The Legacy Continues

The life of Anna Knight cannot be summed up in a few words written on the pages of this book. The things you do for yourself are gone when you are gone, but the things you have done for others remain your legacy. Many people and organizations have recognized her for the contributions that she made in the name of Education. First, the elementary school on the campus of Oakwood College now University, was named in her honor, The Anna Knight Elementary School. Later the school decided to build a larger facility and the old elementary school building became the Anna Knight Education Building, students who plan to enter the field of education classes are held.

In July 1990 the General Conference Session of Seventh-day Adventist was held in Indianapolis, Indiana. The South Atlanta Conference Women's Commission under the leadership of Dr. Deborah Harris held a "Hands Across the Waters" Reception. It was a gathering of women of many cultures, countries, states and denominations coming together in one place. Dr. Harris asked me to create and establish an award in honor of my great aunt Anna Knight. At the event the "Anna Knight Christian Service Award" was announced and unveiled. This award is given to an individual who has demonstrated a great service to the church, education or the community. The beautiful award was designed by James K. Lamb of Atlanta, Georgia.

As mentioned previously in the pages of this book, she was buried in the Newton Knight Cemetery on the Jasper and Jones County line. At the time there was no headstone placed on her grave, just a metal plate with her name, birthdate and the date of her death. The Gulf States Conference of Seventh-day Adventist along with other Conferences placed a beautiful granite carved headstone at her grave. The Anna Knight Memorial Service held among the tall pine trees in the woods at the Knight Family cemetery was on May 28, 2001. A bus filled with representatives of different conferences was present. They included Malcolm Gordon, President of Southern Union, Bruce Peifer, Oakwood College, Joseph McCoy, President of South Central Conference, Mel Eisele, President of Gulf States Conference, and the North American Division President, Don Schneider unveiled the Monument and made the Commitment, Jim Nix from the Ellen G. White Estate was present and the melodious voice of T. Marshall Kelley vibrated through the woods. My sister Florence Blaylock, and cousins, Lois Wilson and Olga Watts and I witnessed this beautiful Memorial Service at Anna Knight's gravesite.

Her life's work was not forgotten by the people of India. Dr. Herold Lee, then President of the Columbia Union with the help of the Columbia Union Conference, Kettering Medical Center and Adventist Health Systems donated funds to build a nurses' Hostel at the Giffard Memorial Hospital in Nuzvid, India. Inspired by the life of Anna Knight, the first black female Christian Missionary nurse who spent six and one-half years teaching, nursing in India, the hospital named the building, the "Anna Knight Nurses Hostel." I was invited by Dr. Herold Lee to travel to India to dedicate the new building. My sister Florence Blaylock went with me. We boarded our flight for the nineteen-hour trip November 2005, arriving at the Giffard Memorial Hospital Campus. There stood a beautiful light yellow building; the workers were placing the final touches to get ready for the dedication service. We visited the hospital which served the people from the nearby villages and anyone who needed medical attention. It was a beautiful sight to see the student nurses and doctors going to the classes and working in the hospital as a part of their training. The dedication ceremony was held November 21, 2005. Florence and I cut the ribbon and unveiled the stone showing the face of Anna Knight etched in it. The students entertained us with a program of cultural dances and songs as an expression of thanks for the new building that will house one hundred female student nurses. The cornerstone carved with the face of this pioneer missionary nurse on the new building reminds us, "That our daughters may be as a corner stone polished after the similitude of a palace."

Not only did she serve the Christian community, she also was a part of the civic activities. In 2009, the Jones County Community College located in Ellisville, Mississippi approached my sister Florence and me with the idea of establishing a scholarship to be named in her honor. Together Jones faculty member Tammy Townsend and humanities chairperson Cheryl Windham established the scholarship. Since then we have solicited additional funds from friends and family to keep the scholarship going in order to serve deserving students. The Anna Knight Memorial Scholarship is designed to provide scholarship assistance to students pursuing a degree in nursing or education. Each year we are proud to award this scholarship to such a student.

The Historic Adventist Village, located in Battle Creek, Michigan has an exhibit profiling the life of Anna Knight. This is in the city where the Battle Creek Sanitarium was located, that she graduated from in 1898. Although the Sanitarium is no longer there because of fire, a new building was erected on the same site in 1928 which served as a hospital and now is a government office building. You can still visit the site of the old hospital and the historical information regarding the hospital is inside. To be included in the Historic Village the place where Ellen G. White's home is located and to be visited by hundreds of people every year is a testament that the legacy of this great pioneering woman will live on.

Working tirelessly over the years trying to keep the memory and the legacy of my great aunt Anna Knight alive was an enjoyable task, but sometimes I did not know what or where to go. I still had all the papers and information in my possession. I called a good friend of mine, Dr. Garland Dulan and told him about my situation and that another University wanted it. He expressed to me in so many words, "her life belongs here at Oakwood University." I think that was the encouragement that made me realize that Oakwood was the place for all her papers and other information. There was already an exhibit of her life in the Clara Peterson Rock Museum on the campus. We met with the President of Oakwood University, Dr. Leslie Pollard and other committee members, and laid out the vision for the establishment of the Anna Knight Center for Women's Leadership, we came to an agreement of what and how the vision could be accomplished. The Anna Knight Center for Women's Leadership will house all the personal papers, documents and reports of her work. We gifted all the information to Oakwood University in 2014. On March 27, 2016, Dr. Leslie N. Pollard, President of Oakwood University dedicated the Anna Knight Center for Women's Leadership. The Center is located in the Eva B. Dykes Library located on the University's campus. This has been work over many years that have finally found a home.

The Knight Family has always been filled with a lot of history. Stories about the Knight Family have been talked about for years, many family members did not want to talk about it because it was complicated for them. A book was written by Victoria Bynum "The Free State of Jones" which is about the father of Anna Knight, Newton Knight who fought in the Civil War and later formed his own Company to fight against the Confederate army. Ms. Bynum did extensive research on the Knight Family. She reviewed the information that we had in our family files and information from others and the book caught the attention of Hollywood producer Gary Ross. The life of Newton Knight was a fascinating story and would make an exciting movie the producer thought. So now we have it, the movie, "The Free State of Jones" starring Matthew McConaughey, a well-known actor, portraying Newton Knight. The movie was released in 2016. Some of the family members both on the black and white side of the family had small parts in the movie. My sister and I had the privilege of having a small part. It was an exciting adventure for us.

As I mentioned before, her legacy and the life of the Knight family will take many paths for the good of the people whom she served. This bi-racial young lady from the deep south of Mississippi grew up to do great and wonderful work in spite of the many obstacles that were put in her way. Yes, Aunt Anna, you have proven that "green things do grow."

Just the Sand

Just the sand filtering down
the stream to the valley below
The sweet flowing bays of the
Magnolia trees swaying gently
among the tall strong pine trees
A land of paradise with its
fertile soil, abundance of wild game
and a wealth of possibilities
In the middle of all the beauty
was the "Mississippi Girl" who had
"Just the Sand"

By Dorothy Knight Marsh

Resources

1. Gospel Herald, Volume V. #3, March 3 1908, Nashville, Tenn.
2. The Adventist Review and Herald, June 6, 1912
3. Interview with Clarence C. Crisler, Atlanta, Georgia, July 5, 1913
4. Interview with Mr. Spaulding, Atlanta, Georgia, November 19, 1914
5. National Colored Teachers Association By-Laws 1922
6. Letter from Mrs. Mary S. Foy, February 3, 1931
7. Letter from W. K. Kellogg, Bessie Strong Secretary to W.K Kellogg February 5, 1931
8. Letter to Mary S Foy, Battle Creek Sanitarium, Battle Creek, Michigan February 10, 1931
9. Article written by Anna Knight "The Hope of the Race" personal papers
10. Speech by Anna Knight, personal papers.
11. Spreading Oak, Oakwood College, and March, 1951.
12. Personal letters to and from family, notes and diaries
13. The Mississippi Girl, Anna Knight's Autobiography, published in 1952 Southern Publishing Association, Nashville, Tennessee
14. Medallion of Merit Award Program, Oakwood College, 1971 Anna Knights Personal papers

15. South Atlantic Conference Women's Commission, "Hands Across the Waters Program, General Conference Session, Indianapolis, Indiana, July 12, 1990

16. Adventist Review, October 18, 1984 Article by Lois B. Rey

17. Photos from Anna Knight personal collection.

Chronology of Anna Knight

March 4, 1874
Born to Newton and Georgeann Knight in Jasper County, Mississippi.

1891
Learns about Seventh-day Adventist from Ida Embree, of Sign of the Times, and W. W. Eastman, a colporteur in Texas.

1892
I. Dyo Chambers of Chattanooga, Tennessee prepares Anna for baptism. Baptized into the Adventist faith.

1894
Mr. and Mrs. Chambers teach Anna at home. Enrolled into Mt. Vernon Academy, Mt. Vernon Ohio.

1898
Graduates from Battle Creek Sanitarium Training School, as a self-supporting Missionary Nurse
Battle Creek, Michigan.

1898-1901
Returns to Mississippi. Establishes School for the children in the Knight community.

1901
Attends General Conference Session in Battle Creek, Michigan, Volunteers for missionary service to India as a nurse.

1901 – May 26
Leaves for Calcutta, India. Traveled with Elder and Mrs. J.L. Shaw, Elder G. K. Owens and Miss Donna Humphrey.

1901 – June 28
Arrives in Calcutta, India, Howrah Railroad Station.

1901-1902
Worked Sanitariums in Calcutta and Karmatar Mission.

1902- April
Worked in Simla India for summer, Delhi, India with co-worker Donna Humphrey.

1903- March 4th
Donna Humphreys dies.

1907-November
Anna returns to America from India on a two-year furlough. Stopped in Washington, DC visited Mrs. Irwin. Visited Graysville, TN spoke at the local church twice before continuing home to Mississippi. Rebuild and reopen the school in Gitano. Trained her sister Grace to teach in the school.

1907-1909
Worked part-time as a Bible Worker for the Mississippi Conference.

1909-
Called to Atlanta, Georgia to open a colored sanitarium as serve as medical matron. Grace, her sister continued teaching the school in Gitano. Anna taught night classes in the local churches.

1913
Organized the first colored Young Women's Christian Association (YWCA) in Atlanta, Georgia.

1913 – July 5th
Clarence C. Chrisler interviews Anna Knight in Atlanta, Georgia

1909-1915
Served as Church Leader for the Colored Department of the Southeastern Union and Georgia Cumberland Conferences.

1915- 1920
Served as Home Missionary Leader, Young People's Missionary Volunteer Secretary, Educational Secretary and served on the Oakwood College Board under President Elder J. Tucker.

1920 – 1926
Anna Knight served as Home Missionary Leader, and Young People Missionary Volunteer for the Southern Union.

1922
Anna served as the first president of the National Colored Teachers Association.

1922- Summer
Teaches Denominational History and Spirit Prophecy at Oakwood College.

1926
Served as Home Missionary Leader, Young People's Missionary Volunteer Secretary, and Educational Secretary for the Southeastern Union Conference.

1934 – May 25-28
Hosts the first Colored Youth Congress sponsored by the General Conference of SDA on the Oakwood Junior College Campus.

1932 – 1946
Served as Associate Secretary for the Home Missionary, Young People's Missionary Volunteer and Education Secretary for the Greater Southern Union Conference.

1945
Served on Colored Survey Committee to help establish the South Atlantic and South Central Conferences.

1946
Anna Knight Retires at the age of 72 years moves to Oakwood College.

1952
Publishes her autobiography, *Mississippi Girl.*

1961 – May 2nd
The Pi Lambda Sigma Honor Society awards Anna the Award of Merit.

1971- November 17th
Awarded the Medallion of Merit by General Conference of Seventh-day Adventist Education Department. She was the thirteenth person to receive the award.

<u>1972 – June 3rd</u>

Anna Knight dies at the age of ninety-eight, Riverside Hospital in Nashville, TN.

<u>1972- June 8th</u>

Funeral Services held in Moran Hall at Oakwood College, Huntsville, AL.

<u>1972 – June 10th</u>

Buried in the Newton Knight Cemetery, near Six Town, Mississippi.